Frommer's®

Berlin
day BY day™

2nd Edition

by Kerry Christiani

WILEY

A John Wiley and Sons, Ltd, Publication

Contents

Copyright © 2012 John Wiley & Sons Ltd,
The Atrium, Southern Gate, Chichester,
West Sussex PO19 8SQ, England
Telephone (+44) 1243 779777
Email (for orders and customer service enquiries): cs-books@wiley.co.uk. Visit
our Home Page on www.wiley.com

Editorial Director: Kelly Regan
Production Manager: Daniel Mersey
Commissioning Editor: Mark Henshall
Development Editor: Jill Emeny
Content Editor: Erica Peters
Photo Research: Jill Emeny
Cartography: Simonetta Giori

Wiley also publishes its books in a variety of electronic formats and by print-
on-demand. Some content that appears in standard print versions of this book
may not be available in other formats. For more information about Wiley prod-
ucts, visit us at www.wiley.com.

British Library Cataloguing in Publication Data

A catalogue record for this book is available from the British Library

ISBN 978-1-119-99318-6 (pbk), ISBN 978-1-119-97255-6 (ebk),
ISBN 978-1-119-99452-7 (ebk), ISBN 978-1-119-99468-8 (ebk)

Typeset by Wiley Indianapolis Composition Services

Printed and bound in China by RR Donnelley

5 4 3 2 1

A Note from the Editorial Director

Organizing your time. That's what this guide is all about.

Other guides give you long lists of things to see and do and then expect you to fit the pieces together. The Day by Day guides are different. These guides tell you the best of everything, and then they show you how to see it *in the smartest, most time-efficient way*. Our authors have designed detailed itineraries organized by time, neighborhood, or special interest. And each tour comes with a bulleted map that takes you from stop to stop.

Hoping to view the city from Reichstag, watch the Brandenburg gate lit up at night or see some art on a stretch of the Berlin Wall? Planning to roam the cobbled lanes of medieval Nikolaiviertel, stride through the green Tiergarten, jump in an iconic Trabi or just munch on *Currywurst* and take in the scene? Whatever your interest or schedule, the Day by Days give you the smartest routes to follow. Not only do we take you to the top attractions, hotels, and restaurants, but we also help you access those special moments that locals get to experience—those "finds" that turn tourists into travelers.

The Day by Days are also your top choice if you're looking for one complete guide for all your travel needs. The best hotels and restaurants for every budget, the greatest shopping values, the wildest nightlife—it's all here.

Why should you trust our judgment? Because our authors personally visit each place they write about. They're an independent lot who say what they think and would never include places they wouldn't recommend to their best friends. They're also open to suggestions from readers. If you'd like to contact them, please send your comments our way at feedback@frommers.com, and we'll pass them on.

Enjoy your Day by Day guide—the most helpful travel companion you can buy. And have the trip of a lifetime.

Warm regards,

Kelly Regan

Kelly Regan, Editorial Director
Frommer's Travel Guides

About the Author

Award-winning travel writer **Kerry Christiani** (www.kerrychristiani.com) has lived in Germany and written about it for the past 6 years. From her home in the Black Forest it's a speedy train ride to Berlin, where the dynamic arts scene, fun-loving locals and happening nightlife draw her back time and again. This was Kerry's second trip to Berlin for Frommer's, but the first time she has seen the capital entirely blanketed in snow, and toasted the New Year with champagne and fireworks at the Brandenburg Gate. When she isn't digging up treasures for guidebooks, Kerry writes articles for magazines and websites, including BBC *Olive* and *Lonely Planet Magazine.*

About the Photographer

Born and based in the Black Forest, **Andy Christiani** (www.andychristiani.com) is a freelance photographer. His father Hans—a true Berliner—sparked his curiosity with the German capital at a young age. Andy's work has been widely published in guidebooks, magazines and newspapers, both in print and online. His photography also illustrates the award-winning *Marrakech Day by Day.*

Acknowledgments

Huge thanks to everyone who made this guide possible on what was a bitterly cold and very snowy research trip. A special thank you to Michel Henri for the generous loan of his (warm) Charlottenburg apartment. Big thanks to Stefan Heulle at Deutsche Bahn for his assistance, to William Liebscher and Christian Tänzler at Berlin Tourismus & Kongress GmbH for their help, and to Silvester in Berlin GmbH.

Advisory & Disclaimer

The inclusion of a company, organization or Website in this guide as a service provider and/or potential source of further information does not mean that we endorse them or the information they provide. Be aware that information provided through some Websites may be unreliable and can change without notice. Neither the publisher or author shall be liable for any damages arising herefrom.

Ratings, Icons & Abbreviations

Every hotel, restaurant, and attraction listing in this guide has been ranked for quality, value, service, amenities, and special features using a **star-rating system.** Hotels, restaurants, attractions, shopping, and nightlife are rated on a scale of zero stars (recommended) to three stars (exceptional). In addition to the star-rating system, we also use a **kids icon** to point out the best bets for families. Within each tour, we recommend cafes, bars, or restaurants where you can take a break with a € sign to indicate price. Each of these stops appears in a shaded box marked with a coffee-cup-shaped bullet ☕.

The following **abbreviations** are used for credit cards:

| AE | American Express | DISC | Discover | V | Visa |
| DC | Diners Club | MC | MasterCard | | |

Travel Resources at Frommers.com

Frommer's travel resources don't end with this guide. Frommer's website, **www.frommers.com**, has travel information on more than 4,000 destinations. We update features regularly, giving you access to the most current trip-planning information and the best airfare, lodging, and car-rental bargains. You can also listen to podcasts, connect with other Frommers.com members through our active-reader forums, share your travel photos, read blogs from guidebook editors and fellow travelers, and much more.

How to Contact Us

In researching this book, we discovered many wonderful places—hotels, restaurants, shops, and more. We're sure you'll find others. Please tell us about them, so we can share the information with your fellow travelers in upcoming editions. If you were disappointed with a recommendation, we'd love to know that, too. Please e-mail: frommers@wiley.com or write to:

Frommer's Berlin Day by Day, 2nd Edition
John Wiley & Sons, Inc. • 111 River St. • Hoboken, NJ 07030-5774

15 Favorite
Moments

15 Favorite **Moments**

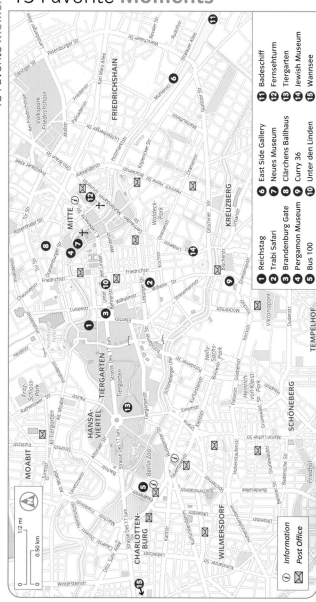

Information

Post Office

Previous page: Nikolaiviertel.

"Berlin is poor, but sexy," quipped Mayor Klaus Wowereit, and it's true. Debt may be sky-high, but the trendsetting, party-loving German capital knows how to show visitors a good time. Whether you go for Museum Island's world-renowned galleries, an arty tour of the Wall, or Friedrichshain's pulsating nightlife, Berlin will excite and entertain you. Here are my 15 favorite moments.

1 **Zooming up to the Reichstag's futuristic cupola.** Book an early-morning tour of Norman Foster's glass dome. Ascend the spiral ramp to a platform that affords far-reaching vistas over Berlin, from the Brandenburg Gate to the Siegessäule. *See p 7.*

2 **Getting wild behind the wheel of a Trabi.** Go, Trabi, go! Pick your dream machine, pull the choke, and feel your two-stroke splutter past landmarks from the Fernsehturm to the monumental Karl-Marx-Allee. These cult GDR cars are the coolest way to enjoy the sights of Berlin's "Wild East." *See p 53.*

3 **Gazing on the Brandenburg Gate by night.** The Gate is always mesmerizing, but all the more so when light bathes its Doric columns and quadriga in gold. Dusk is the best time to snap the triumphal arch and soak up the style of Pariser Platz, with its dancing fountains and street entertainers. *See p 7.*

4 **Going back to Babylon at the Pergamon Museum.** Early risers can beat the crowds to view Berlin's treasure-trove of antiquities. Admire friezes of burly Greek gods as you scale the marble steps to the Pergamon Altar. Then step over to Babylon to pick out mythical unicorns on the Ishtar Gate. *See p 8.*

5 **Taking a self-guided city tour on bus 100.** Take a seat on the top deck of bus 100 for a "greatest hits" tour of Berlin. The route from Zoologischer Garten to Alexanderplatz is a brilliant introduction to the city, taking in the golden Siegessäule

Gazing upon the Brandenburg Gate by night.

(p 13), the Brandenburg Gate (p 7), and Fernsehturm (p 49). *See p 13.*

6 **Walking the Wall at the East Side Gallery.** Vibrant graffiti, from a crashing Trabant to the politically charged *Bruderkuss* (Brotherly Kiss), always captures my imagination at this unique stretch of Berlin Wall. The open-air gallery offers an insight into a once-divided city, and a brush with its creative side. *See p 15.*

7 **Marveling at Nefertiti in the Neues Museum.** Berlin's new flagship museum is a magnificent voyage into Ancient Egypt. Be transported back 4,000 years, contemplating intricate tomb friezes and mummy masks. In room 21, the bust of beautiful queen Nefertiti is spellbinding. *See p 68.*

8 **Partying like its 1929.** Throw yourself into Berlin's glamorous 1920s revival and dance the Charleston at a Bohème Sauvage club night. Or find out why ballroom is hip again

Seven Steps to Enlightenment, East Side Gallery.

at Wednesday swing night at Clärchens Ballhaus. *See p 43.*

9 Munching *Currywurst* at Curry 36. No trip to Berlin would be complete without a bite of the legendary *Currywurst* (curried sausage). Join the line in Kreuzberg to sink your teeth into this spicy snack. Just the smell of it makes me hungry. *See p 16.*

10 Sauntering down Unter den Linden. Bankrolled by Prussian royalty, Unter den Linden is Berlin's showcase boulevard. History unfolds as you take in the grand monuments and museums, from the triumphal Brandenburg Gate to the Deutsches Historisches Museum. *See p 8.*

11 Chilling on Badeschiff. On hot summer days, few things beat hanging out with Kreuzberg's cool crowd at this floating container ship on the River Spree. Berliners gather to crunch sand between their toes, take a dip in the pool, and sip daiquiris as DJs spin R'n'B tunes till late. *See p 126.*

12 Orbiting above the city at Fernsehturm. Catch sweeping views of the city from its most visible landmark. Rising above Alexanderplatz is this enormous golf ball,

skewered on a needle-thin spike. *See p 49.*

13 Striding through Tiergarten. Berlin's green center is best explored on foot. When the sun's out, I join locals to recline under the willows, picnic on the banks of the Spree, or quench my thirst in a leafy beer garden. Kids in tow? Take them to see the giant panda and other loveable animals at Berlin Zoo. *See p 97.*

14 Revisiting the past at the Jewish Museum. Daniel Libeskind's lightning-bolt creation whisks you on a journey through Jewish-German life. From walking the eerie Memory Void to the isolation of the Holocaust Tower, this museum unleashes emotions that stretch from horror to admiration. *See p 16.*

15 Building sandcastles at Wannsee. There's no sea for miles, but Berlin does have its own sandy beach on the banks of Wannsee. The city's bustle fades as you kick back in a *Strandkorb* (wicker lounger), devour ice cream, and watch the yachts bob. On clear days, the sunsets are bewitching. *See p 100.* ●

The Best of Berlin **in One Day**

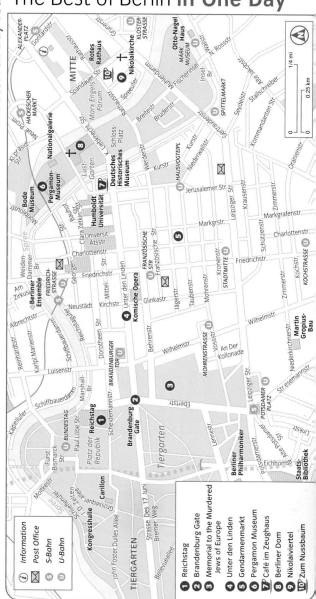

Legend:
- ⓘ Information
- ⊠ Post Office
- Ⓢ S-Bahn
- Ⓤ U-Bahn

1. Reichstag
2. Brandenburg Gate
3. Memorial to the Murdered Jews of Europe
4. Unter den Linden
5. Gendarmenmarkt
6. Pergamon Museum
7. Café im Zeughaus
8. Berliner Dom
9. Nikolaiviertel
10. Zum Nussbaum

Previous page: Gendarmenmarkt.

This whirlwind tour takes in Berlin's trophy sights from the glass dome crowning the Reichstag to a classic saunter down the Unter den Linden boulevard. After a brief detour to Ancient Greece at the Pergamon Museum, you can catch a memorable sunset by the River Spree and toast your first day with a cool Berliner Kindl in Zum Nussbaum. START: **U-Bahn to Bundestag.**

1 ★★★ Reichstag. Start your day with a visit to the Reichstag (Germany's parliament) for a captivating view over the city. A lift rises to architect Norman Foster's striking glass cupola, which revamped Berlin's architectural landscape in 1999. There's nothing like the moment you step inside the kaleidoscopic shell, where a mirrored funnel creates an optical illusion; it's like being trapped inside a giant glass spider's web. The 360° panorama of Berlin from the platform is ideal for getting your bearings. Check the website for details on guided tours and do book in advance. ⏱ *20–90 min. Platz der Republik 1.* ☎ *030-22-73-21-52. www.bundestag.de. Free admission. Tours daily 10:30am, 1:30, 5:30 & 6:30pm when parliament is not sitting; advance booking essential. U-Bahn: Bundestag.*

A close-up view of Sir Norman Foster's glass cupola at Reichstag.

The Doric columns of the Brandenburg Gate soar above Platz des 18 März.

2 ★★★ Brandenburg Gate. In 1987, Ronald Reagan stood at this spot and cried: "Mr Gorbachev, open this gate! Mr Gorbachev, tear down this wall!" And 2 years later, he did. Just a few paces from the Reichstag, the Doric columns of the Brandenburg Gate stop you dead in your tracks. Crane your neck to glimpse Victoria, goddess of victory, charging forth on her two-wheeled chariot, quadriga. Conquering French Emperor Napoleon took a fancy to his feisty beauty in 1804 and whisked her off to the Louvre in Paris; rather fittingly, she now stands triumphant above Pariser Platz (Paris Square). Return here at dusk to see the neoclassical landmark at its most photogenic. ⏱ *20 min. Pariser Platz 1. U-Bahn: Brandenburger Tor.*

3 ★★ Memorial to the Murdered Jews of Europe. This

A field of gray stelae at Peter Eisenman's labyrinthine Holocaust Memorial.

life-size jigsaw puzzle pieces together Berlin's troubled past. Peter Eisenman, born in New Jersey in 1932, completed this monument to commemorate the murdered Jews of Europe in 2005. Enter the concrete labyrinth at any point and you soon feel lost: row upon row of wavy *stelae* (upright stone slabs) appear to ripple off to infinity. On a gray winter's day, it is chilling yet beautiful in its austerity. Be sure to visit the **Ort der Information** (Information Center), particularly room 3, which reveals the identity of many Holocaust victims. ⏲ *30 min. Cora-Berliner-Strasse 1.* ☎ *030-26-39-43-36. www.holocaust-mahnmal.de. Free admission; donations welcome. Information Center Apr–Sept daily 10am–8pm; Oct–Mar daily 10am–7pm. U-Bahn: Brandenburger Tor.*

❹ ★★★ kids **Unter den Linden.** Watch daily life unfold as you stroll along this monumental avenue. Flanked by linden trees—which Germans nickname *Bäume der Liebe* (trees of love) because of their heart-shaped leaves—this is Berlin's show-piece boulevard. The clip-clop of horses recalls the days when it was a bridle path for Prussian kings. Look out for the marble facade of the Russian Embassy, the vine-clad courtyard of the Staatsbibliothek zu Berlin (Berlin State Library), and Humboldt University, where Einstein taught. ⏲ *45 min. U-Bahn: Brandenburger Tor.*

❺ ★★ **Gendarmenmarkt.** Take a right off Unter den Linden onto Berlin's grandest square and try to

figure out what's unusual—you may soon realize you are seeing double. Gendarmenmarkt is dwarfed by the baroque Deutscher Dom and Französischer Dom, two churches that are the spitting image of each other (both built in 1705). At the center of the square, German poet Friedrich Schiller (1759–1805) rises proudly in front of the columned Konzerthaus. The square is fringed by cafes and glorious Art Nouveau townhouses (number 38 is a fine example). When the evening sun hits the cobbled streets it's as if they are, quite literally, paved with gold. ⏲ *45 min. Gendarmenmarkt. U-Bahn: Französische Strasse.*

❻ ★★★ **Pergamon Museum.** This cavernous treasure-trove presents a romp through Ancient Greece, Rome, and Babylon. Though its scale is overwhelming, some of the most impressive exhibits are located in one area. You start in the Antiquities Collection, harboring the original-size, reconstructed Pergamon Altar, which catapults you back to 160 B.C. Greece with its frieze of burly gods doing battle with the Titans. Steep marble steps lead to the Altar Court, where sacrificial rituals took place in the 2nd century B.C. If you can tear yourself away from Athens, pop next door to Babylon to marvel at a gate fit for an Assyrian goddess—with glazed tiles depicting mythical creatures. Step back to appreciate the gate's magnitude. ⏲ *1½ hr. Am Kupfergraben 5.* ☎ *030-20-90-55-77. www.smb.spk-berlin.de. Admission 10€ adults, 5€*

students, free for children under 18. Daily 10am–6pm, Thurs until 10pm. U-Bahn: Friedrichstrasse.

7 ★ Located within the Deutsches Historisches Museum, the galleried **Café im Zeughaus** fuses old and new with its high ceilings, vibrant floral motifs, and antique-styled chairs. Enjoy coffee and cake or well-prepared German specialties like beef goulash with dumplings. Open in summer, the terrace affords prime views of the Berliner Dom. *Deutsches Historisches Museum, Under den Linden 2. ☎ 030-20-64-27-44. €.*

Café im Zeughaus.

8 ★★★ **Berliner Dom.** This neo-Renaissance cathedral built in 1895 grabs your attention; its graceful cupolas stand in stark contrast to the Fernsehturm (Television Tower) in the background. The centerpiece is a 70m (230 ft.) dome and each of the Dom's intricate mosaics (depicting Biblical scenes) is inlaid with 500,000 stones in myriad colors. For a different perspective, climb 267 steps to the upper gallery where the view stretches across Museumsinsel to the Reichstag and Rotes Rathaus

The Hohenzollern coat of arms in the crypt of the Berliner Dom.

(Red Town Hall). ⏱ *45 min. Am Lustgarten 1. ☎ 030-20-26-91-36. www.berlinerdom.de. Admission 5€ adults, 3€ students, free for children under 14. Mon–Sat 9am–8pm, Sun noon–8pm. U-Bahn: Friedrichstrasse.*

9 ★★ **kids Nikolaiviertel.** Edging south, the laid-back Nikolaiviertel quarter on the banks of the River Spree is a great escape from the central bustle, with cobbled lanes and hidden courtyards to explore. Allow at least an hour to walk around its cafes and boutiques. For unique teas, visit **Teeladen** (p 92). Note the enamel signs above many shops: A pipe for the tobacconist, a pretzel for the baker. Dominating the square is the twin-spired, 13th-century Nikolaikirche (p 157, **2**). ⏱ *45 min. U-Bahn: Alexanderplatz.*

10 ★★ **Zum Nussbaum.** Once the sun starts setting, kick back with a beer on the nut-tree-shaded terrace at one of Berlin's oldest watering holes. Right opposite Nikolaikirche, this bar oozes historic charm in rooms filled with chatter and whiffs of Berliner Eisbein (pork knuckles). *Am Nussbaum 3. ☎ 030-242-30-95. €.*

The Best Full-Day Tours

The Best of Berlin **in Two Days**

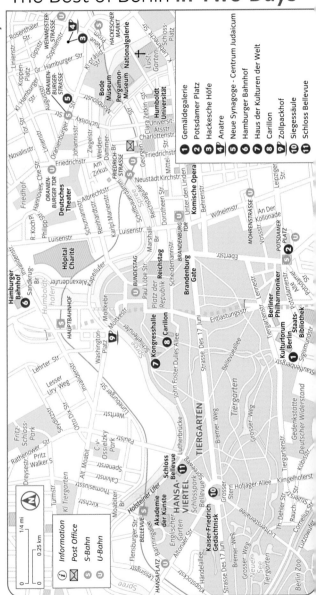

1 Gemäldegalerie
2 Potsdamer Platz
3 Hackesche Höfe
4 Anatre
5 Neue Synagoge – Centrum Judaicum
6 Hamburger Bahnhof
7 Haus der Kulturen der Welt
8 Carillon
9 Zollpackhof
10 Siegessäule
11 Schloss Bellevue

ℹ Information
☒ Post Office
Ⓢ S-Bahn
Ⓤ U-Bahn

0   0.25 km
0   1/4 mi

On your second day, make an early-morning date with Rembrandt, peruse boutique shops, and be drawn to the glint-ing Moorish-style dome of the Neue Synagoge. Take in the pop-art at Hamburger Bahnhof before a leisurely afternoon in Tiergarten, where you'll discover landmarks recalling Berlin's regal past as part of the Kingdom of Prussia (1701–1918). START: **S-Bahn to Potsdamer Platz.**

① ★★★ **Gemäldegalerie.** Housing works by Raphael, Caravaggio, Vermeer, and Rubens, this vast repository of European art is like a who's who of Old Masters. Get here early and target the biggies, such as Jan Vermeer's emotive *The Glass of Wine* (1658) and Jan van Eyck's *Madonna in a Church* (1437–39). In the center of the gallery is an octagonal room dedicated to the handsome brushwork of Dutch Golden Age master Rembrandt van Rijn (1606–69). Among his 16 paintings is *Susanna and the Elders* (1647), which took a staggering 10 years to complete. ⏱ *1 hr. Matthäikirchplatz 4/6.* ☎ *030-266-42-30-40. Admission 8€ adults, 4€ students, free for children under 18. Tues–Sun 10am–6pm, Thurs until 10pm. S-Bahn: Potsdamer Platz.*

The high-rises looming above Potsdamer Platz reflect 21st-century Berlin.

② ★★ 🧒 **Potsdamer Platz.** Potsdamer Platz is Berlin's miniature Manhattan, the city's commercial hub with a round-the-clock buzz and skyscrapers. Prominent sights are the redbrick Kollhoff, boasting Europe's fastest elevator (p 48), the crescent-shaped Deutsche Bank building, and the spinning Mercedes-Benz sign. The most eye-catching building, though, is the crystalline Sony Center (p 89), sheltering restaurants and a cinema beneath a tent-like glass roof. For a taste of how the square looked when divided (before 1989), check out the graffitied fragments of the Berlin Wall in front of the S-Bahn station. ⏱ *1 hr. S-Bahn: Potsdamer Platz.*

③ ★★ **Hackesche Höfe.** A snippet of turn-of-the-century Berlin, these interlinked courtyards are ideal for strolling, boutique shopping, and people-watching. Art Nouveau-style Hof I is the most attractive, with ornamental mosaic walls and curvaceous windows. Roam the other courtyards to bag unique gifts from handmade soaps to vintage jewelry. By night, discover vibrant bars and theaters such as the Chamäleon Varieté (p 135). ⏱ *1 hr. Hackesche Höfe. www.hackesche-hoefe.com. S-Bahn: Hackescher Markt.*

4 ★ **Anatre.** Grab an espresso and snack at this cafe, taking a seat in the patio facing the prettiest courtyard in Hackesche Höfe. The ciabatta sandwiches and antipasti are delicious. Hof I. ☎ 030-28-38-99-15. €.

5 ★★★ **Neue Synagoge–Centrum Judaicum.** Crowned by a shimmering Star of David, this neo-Byzantine synagogue, originally built in 1866, was inspired by Andalusia's Alhambra Palace. The building's trio of bulbous domes feature intricate gold ribbing and appear to glow in the dusk light. The permanent exhibition spotlights Jewish life in Berlin, including the history of the synagogue, while the cupola affords fine views of the hip Scheunenviertel neighborhood, traditionally the city's Jewish quarter. ⏱ 20 min. Oranienburger Strasse 28–30. ☎ 030-88-02-84-51. Admission 3.50€ adults, 2.50€ concessions. Tues–Thurs 10am–6pm, Fri 10am–5pm, Sun–Mon 10am–8pm; closes 2pm on Fri Oct–Mar, closed Sat. S-Bahn: Oranienburger Strasse.

6 ★★ **Hamburger Bahnhof.** With its twin clock towers, graceful arches, and echoing halls, there's no hiding the fact that this gallery was once a train station. The superior collection of contemporary art housed

See the curvaceous domes of the Neue Synagogue blush at dusk.

Henry Moore's Big Butterfly sculpture in front of the Haus der Kulturen der Welt.

here includes works by 20th-century Pop Art stars Andy Warhol and Roy Lichtenstein. Keep an eye out for Warhol's silk-screen of Chairman Mao (1975), Joseph Beuys' classic Tram Stop (1976), and Damien Hirst's pharmaceutical frenzy The Void (2000), exhibiting hundreds of pills in kaleidoscopic shades of color. There are free guided tours in English at noon on Saturday and Sunday. ⏱ 1 hr. Invalidenstrasse 50–51. ☎ 030-39-78-34-11. www.hamburgerbahnhof.de. Admission 12€ adults, 6€ concessions, free for children under 18. Tues–Fri 10am–6pm, Sat 11am–8pm, Sun 11am–6pm. S-Bahn: Hauptbahnhof.

7 ★★ **Haus der Kulturen der Welt.** Whether or not you agree with locals that this contemporary arts center resembles a schwangere Auster (pregnant oyster), there's certainly something shell-like about it. The venue is best surveyed from the front, where the Spiegelteich pond mirrors the edifice; the rippled reflection gives you the sense of being underwater. Have your camera handy for the shimmering centerpiece—British artist Henry Moore's bronze sculpture, Big Butterfly (1984). ⏱ 30 min. John-Foster-Dulles-Allee 10. S-Bahn: Hauptbahnhof.

8 ★★ **kids Carillon.** The oyster's lesser-known neighbor is this 42m (138 ft.) carillon (free-standing bell

On the Buses

Save your spending money with a self-guided city tour on public double-decker bus route 100, running every 7 minutes between Zoologischer Garten and Alexanderplatz. For the price of a single ticket (2.30€ adults, 1.40€ children under 14), you can take in many of Berlin's most iconic sights, including Tiergarten's Siegessäule (below) and Schloss Bellevue (below). Keep an eye out for landmarks such as the Reichstag (p 7), Brandenburg Gate (p 7), and Fernsehturm (p 49) as you trundle through the Mitte district. Grab a seat at the front of the upper deck for the best views. For more ticket information on Berlin's buses, see p 169.

tower) of smooth black granite. Containing 68 bells, the glockenspiel is the world's fourth largest. Continue your stroll through the adjacent sculpture garden. This serene park is a great approach to the **Reichstag** (p 7, **1**), as the open surroundings amplify its dimensions. 🕐 *15 min. Concerts May–Sept Sun 3pm.* ☎ *030-851-28-28. Free public access. S-Bahn: Hauptbahnhof.*

Victoria stands proud atop Siegessäule – Berliners call her Golden Else.

📷 ★★ Zollpackhof. Cold beer, a chestnut-shaded garden, and some of the finest views of Haus der Kulturen der Welt this side of the Spree keep locals and tourists coming back for more. *Elizabeth-Abegg-Strasse 1.* ☎ *030-33-09-97-20. €.*

10 ★★★ kids Siegessäule. The Siegessäule (Victory Column) pops up like a gigantic telescope, and hits you in a wow-I'm-in-Berlin kind of way. Its most defining feature is the angelic Victoria, the same figure crowning the **Brandenburg Gate** (p 7), whose golden wings frame the sky. The memorial commemorates

victory in the 1864 Danish-Prussian war, with reliefs depicting scenes of this battle and two others: the 19th-century Franco-Prussian and Austro-Prussian wars. Puff up 285 steps to the platform for far-reaching views over Berlin. 🕐 *30 min. Grosser Stern 1.* ☎ *030-391-29-61. Admission 2.50€ adults, 1.50€ concessions, free for children under 6. Apr–Oct Mon–Fri 9:30am–6:30pm, Sat–Sun 9:30am–7pm; Nov–Mar Mon–Fri 10am–5pm. S-Bahn: Bellevue.*

11 ★★ kids Schloss Bellevue. From the Siegessäule it's a gentle amble to Schloss Bellevue. Manicured lawns guide the eye to this neoclassical palace on the banks of the Spree, which was built as a summer residence for Prince Ferdinand of Prussia in 1786. Today, the German and EU flags flutter in front of the dazzling white facade of the three-winged building, now the official seat of the president of Germany. 🕐 *30 min. Spreeweg. S-Bahn: Bellevue.*

The Best of Berlin **in Three Days**

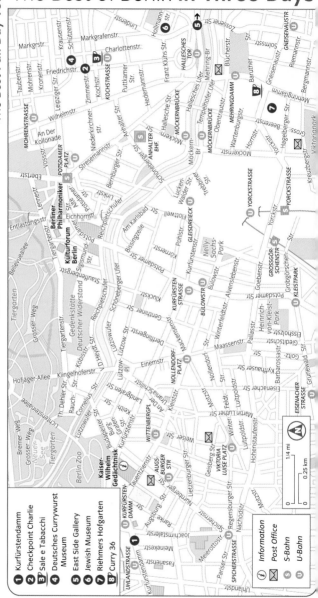

1. Kurfürstendamm
2. Checkpoint Charlie
3. Sale e Tabacchi
4. Deutsches Currywurst Museum
5. East Side Gallery
6. Jewish Museum
7. Riehmers Hofgarten
8. Curry 36

- *i* Information
- ⊠ Post Office
- Ⓢ S-Bahn
- Ⓤ U-Bahn

ay three in Berlin takes you from the elegant boutiques of Kurfürstendamm to edgy Cold War artworks in Friedrichshain. Checkpoint Charlie and the East Side Gallery deserve your undivided attention, as does the highly emotive Jewish Museum. End the day with a spicy *Currywurst* (curried sausage) and fries in Kreuzberg.
START: **U-Bahn to Kurfürstendamm.**

❶ ★★ Kurfürstendamm. Dubbed Ku'damm for short, Berlin's much-loved shopping boulevard is 3½km (2 miles) of chic boutiques, high-street stores, and cafes. Go west toward well-heeled Charlottenburg for designer labels from Gucci to Louis Vuitton; east to Tauentzienstrasse for department stores including **KaDeWe** (don't miss the 6th-floor food court; p 77). Wander the side streets such as Fasanenstrasse and Uhlandstrasse for one-off designs.
🕐 *1½ hr. U-Bahn: Kurfürstendamm.*

❷ ★★ Checkpoint Charlie. From 1961 until the fall of the Wall in 1989, Checkpoint Charlie was the Friedrichstrasse border crossing between East and West Berlin. A replica hut and a soldier's post now mark the former U.S. army checkpoint and there's an open-air exhibition, which gives insight on the Wall and its impact. The adjacent **Mauermuseum** (p 53) tells Berliners'

The soldier's post and replica hut at Checkpoint Charlie.

personal stories of separation and reunification. 🕐 *1 hr. Friedrichstrasse 43–45. U-Bahn: Kochstrasse.*

❸ ★ Sale e Tabacchi. Dark wood paneling and old-fashioned service create a charming setting for a cappuccino or light lunch at this Italian trattoria—the 11.50€ two-course menu of the day represents good value. *Rudi-Dutschke-Strasse 23.* ☎ *030-252-11-55.* €€.

❹ ★ 🅺🅸🅳🆂 Deutsches Currywurst Museum. This hands-on museum is an ode to the humble *Currywurst* (spicy curried sausage), Germany's favorite street snack. You can listen to cult songs about the *wurst*, guess the spices used in the secret curry mix and even get behind the grill yourself. At the front is a snack bar serving—you guessed it—*Currywurst.* 🕐 *45 min. Schützenstrasse 70. Admission 11€ adults, 8.50€ concessions, 7€ children under 13, free for children under 6. Daily 10am–10pm. U-Bahn: Stadtmitte.*

❺ ★★★ East Side Gallery. The name Berlin Wall is a misnomer: In fact it comprised two walls and a corridor, or 'death strip,' where GDR (East German) guards patrolled. Where gray concrete and razor wire once bred fear, people now admire the world's largest open-air gallery (p 56). Stretching 1,300m (4,265 ft.) shadowing the Spree, its colorful graffiti artworks range from politically provocative to fun, and many have a Cold War theme. 🕐 *1 hr.*

Free Berlin Tours

The 3½–hour, English-language walking tours run by New Berlin are a great introduction to the city. Knowledgeable guides take you through Berlin on foot from the Brandenburg Gate to Museum Island, giving some background on sights including the Reichstag, the former SS Headquarters, Bebelplatz, and Checkpoint Charlie. Tours depart daily at 10:30am and 12:30pm in front of Dunkin' Donuts at Zoologischer Garten, and at 9am, 11am, and 1pm by the Brandenburg Gate. It's worth booking ahead online to secure your place. Tours are free, but tips are much appreciated. For more details, visit www.newberlintours.com.

www.eastsidegallery.com. Free admission. S-Bahn: Ostbahnhof.

6 ★★★ **Jewish Museum.** With its dazzling zinc facade, Polish-American architect Daniel Libeskind's brainchild resembles a bolt of lightning. Zigzagging tunnels bring you to the Axis of Holocaust, where the spotlight is on individuals; particularly moving is the toy monkey of a boy whose parents were murdered at Auschwitz. It's scary indeed when the iron door closes, trapping you inside the Holocaust Tower. Other poignant creations include Menashe Kadishman's

Menashe Kadishman's Shalechet (Fallen Leaves) at the Jewish Museum.

Shalechet (Fallen Leaves), a triangular void filled with 10,000 screaming iron faces that clank as you cross them. Upstairs traces German-Jewish life from the Middle Ages to the present. ⏱ *1½ hr. Lindenstrasse 9–14.* ☎ *030-25-99-33-00. www. juedisches-museum-berlin.de. Admission 5€ adults, 2.50€ students, free for children under 6. Mon 10am–10pm, Tues–Sun 10am–8pm. U-Bahn: Hallesches Tor.*

7 ★★ **Riehmers Hofgarten.** Pass through a wrought-iron gate into this Art Nouveau courtyard, a calm retreat in the heart of Kreuzberg. Amble through the chestnut-shaded square to see townhouses draped in vines. It's particularly magical as night falls, when soft lantern light bathes the cobblestoned courtyard. ⏱ *15 min. Yorkstrasse, Hagelberger, and Grossbeerenstrasse. U-Bahn: Mehringdamm.*

8 ★★★ **kids** **Curry 36.** Currywurst is king at this sidewalk joint marked with a red sign. Chow down on your classic Berlin dish with skinny fries or cabbage salad. Be prepared to queue with hungry locals. *Mehringdamm 36. No phone. €.* ●

Something Brewing

1. Café am Neuen See
2. Schleusenkrug
3. Zollpackhof
4. Mommseneck: Haus der 100 Biere
5. Golgatha
6. Heinz Minki
7. Hops & Barley
8. Bier-Spezialitäten-Laden
9. Zur Letzten Instanz
10. Georgbräu
11. Microbrauerei Barkowsky
12. Berliner-Kindl-Schultheiss-Brewery
13. Prater

Previous page: LEGOLAND® Discovery Centre.

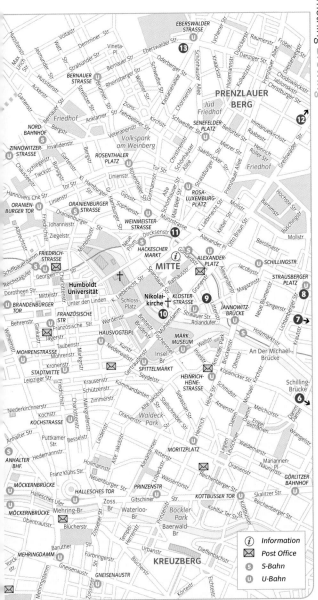

Berlin is no exception in this beer-crazy country. An outing to the capital's lively beer gardens and brewpubs is a great way to slip under Berlin's skin and enjoy homebrews and banter with the locals. So, brace yourself for an intoxicating tour of the top drinking holes: from quaffing under the fruit trees in Kreuzberg to slurping pilsner by the meter in the Nikolaiviertel. START: **S-Bahn to Tiergarten.**

❶ ★ kids Café am Neuen See. Quench your thirst on warm weekends at Berlin's biggest beer garden, seating 1,000. Join beer-guzzling locals on the benches beside this tranquil lake for cool lagers and giant pretzels. A sandpit, table tennis, and rowing boats (5€ for 30 min.) will keep kids amused, for a while anyway. *Lichtensteinallee 2.* ☎ *030-254-49-30. Daily 9 or 10am to 10pm. S-Bahn: Tiergarten.*

❷ Schleusenkrug. Enjoy a leisurely saunter along the **Landwehrkanal** (p 71, ❶) to this canal-front beer garden. The name is a fusion of *Schleuse* (lock) and *Krug* (beer mug). The attractive garden, with its willow and creeping roses, provides respite from the city's bustle and is packed to the gunnels on balmy evenings. The grill rustles up a selection of tasty snacks from 4pm—try the spicy Merguez sausages. *Müller-Breslau-Strasse, Tiergarten.* ☎ *030-313-99-09. May–Sep daily 10am–2am; Oct–Apr Mon–Fri 11am–7pm, Sat–Sun 10am–7pm. S-Bahn: Tiergarten.*

❸ ★ kids Zollpackhof. This effervescent beer garden makes a popular pitstop on the Sunday afternoon trail along tree-fringed **Helgoländer Ufer** (p 59, ❸). The chestnut-shaded garden has fabulous views of the **Haus der Kulturen der Welt** (p 12) and **Bundeskanzleramt** (p 59). It's a great spot to while away happy hours sipping Berliner Weisse mit Schuss (see box, below), and listening to boats chug past, or warming up beside an open fire on chilly days. *Elizabeth-Abegg-Strasse 1.* ☎ *030-33-09-97-20. www. zollpackhof.de. Mar–Oct daily 11am–midnight; Nov–Feb Mon–Fri 10am–6pm, closed Sat–Sun. S-Bahn: Hauptbahnhof.*

❹ Mommseneck: Haus der 100 Biere. Choose from 100 different beers at this gallery-style gastropub on Potsdamer Platz. There are brews from Europe, America, Asia, and Australasia, including 12 on tap. The mind-boggling array includes Berliner Kindl, Jamaican Red Stripe, Guinness, and Japanese Kirin. These are accompanied by old-fashioned

Hire a boat at Café am Neuen See for a different perspective of Tiergarten.

Berliner Weisse mit Schuss

Love it or hate it, when in Berlin you can't avoid the ubiquitous *Berliner Weisse mit Schuss*. This summertime tipple takes Berliner Weisse, a tangy top-fermented beer, and adds a shot of syrup. Choose between raspberry-flavored *Himbeere* or *Waldmeister* with a woodruff (a fragrant herb) kick. Served in a chunky goblet with a straw, the drink is a playful interpretation of one of Berlin's favorite brews, and extremely refreshing if you can cope with the traffic-light shades and strong whiff of syrup. Impress the locals by simply ordering a Berliner Weisse *rot* (red) or *grün* (green).

Berlin dishes such as pea soup with *Bockwurst* (veal sausage) and pork knuckles with sauerkraut. *Alte Potsdamer Strasse.* ☎ *030-25-29-66-35. Daily 11am–midnight. S-Bahn: Pots-damer Platz.*

Berliner Weisse with Himbeere (raspberry syrup) is refreshing in summer.

⑤ ★ Golgatha. In the heart of Kreuzberg's Vik-toriapark, this leafy beer garden becomes an open-air club after 10pm, with DJs spinning electro, rock, and pop. You can come to dance or just for relaxed drinks on the terrace. Top-notch German brews such as Löwenbräu from Munich and the local Kreuzberg Monastery dark beer go well with snacks from the charcoal grill. *Dudenstrasse 40.* ☎ *030-785-24-53. www.golgatha-berlin.de. Apr–Sept daily 10am–6am, closed Oct–Mar. U-Bahn: Platz der Luftbrücke.*

⑥ ★ Heinz Minki. Over the Ober-baumbrücke, and down Schlesische Strasse, stands Heinz Minki (p 130), opening onto a garden enveloped in vines and strung with lanterns. This relaxed Kreuzberg hangout is

Berlin's last remaining tollgate, dating from 1859. Today the enchanting garden, shaded by 100-year-old apple and pear trees, exudes a come-as-you-are feel. Year-round, the 1970s-style bar attracts a lively crowd with regular events from DJs to table football tourna-ments. *Vor dem Schlesischen Tor 3.* ☎ *030-69-53-37-66. www.heinzminki.de. Daily noon–late. U-Bahn: Schlesisches Tor.*

⑦ ★★ Hops & Barley. This friendly, down-to-earth microbrew-ery in Friedrichshain offers up hoppy pilsners, malty dark beers, and refreshing wheat beers.

Rocket pizza at Heinz Minki.

Alternatively, there is also excellent homemade cider on tap, or try a *Schlangenbiss* (snake bite), a beer and cider mix with a shot of blackcurrant. You can snack on *Treberbrot*, hearty bread made with spent grain, and sausage. *Wühlischstrasse 22–23.* ☎ *030-29-36-75-34. Daily 5pm–3am. U-Bahn: Samariterstrasse.*

⑧ Bier-Spezialitäten-Laden. This hole-in-the-wall store in Friedrichshain stocks 500 beers from all over the world, including German *Rauchbier* (smoked beer) and Belgian *Kriekbier* (cherry beer). It's also where Berliners come for take-away local brews such as top-fermented Berliner Weisse. You can even buy the glasses to match. *Karl-Marx-Allee 56.* ☎ *030-249-21-46. Mon–Fri 10am–7:30pm, Sat 10am–2:30pm, closed Sun. U-Bahn: Strausberger Platz.*

⑨ ★★ kids Zur Letzten Instanz. Berlin's oldest inn, dating back to 1621, Zur Letzten Instanz (To the Last Instance) provides a cozy atmosphere, hearty local fare, and fine brews in wood-paneled surrounds. Napoleon Bonaparte once supped beside the tiled stove, now graced with a bust of the French emperor. Sharp-witted waiters serve classics from pickled pork knuckles to meatballs, but if you're feeling adventurous I recommend the *Anwalts Frühstück* (Lawyer's Breakfast)—a

Pull up a chair for hearty German fare at Zur Letzten Instanz, Berlin's oldest inn.

pair of blood sausages with creamed sauerkraut and parsley. *Waisenstrasse 14–16.* ☎ *030-242-55-28. www.zurletzteninstanz.de. Mon–Sat noon–1am. U-Bahn: Alexanderplatz.*

⑩ Georgbräu. After boutique shopping in the Nikolaiviertel (p 64), put your feet up at this congenial microbrewery. The shady terrace by the Spree overlooks a bronze of St George slaying the dragon by sculptor August Kiss (circa 1856). Inside shining copper vats and dark wood create a warm ambiance for serious beer drinking. If you're thirsty, order a pitcher of the home-brewed Georg Pils or go the whole hog with a meter of beer (roughly 12 glasses). Pork is

Roll out the Barrel

If your appetite has been whetted, time your visit for the free **Berlin International Beer Festival** (☎ 030-65-76-35-60; www. bierfestival-berlin.de). On the first weekend in August, monumental Karl-Marx-Allee morphs into the world's largest beer garden, tempting ale lovers with some 2,000 different brews from 86 countries. Drink in the party atmosphere on the 2.2km (1.3 miles) route with steins a-swinging and folk music on 18 stages from Frankfurter Tor to Strausberger Platz.

Top German Beers

Get versed in German beer before you hit Berlin's brewpubs and beer gardens. Many of the best beers are still brewed according to the centuries-old purity law, and are made with just water, hops, barley and yeast.

Pilsner, or Pils for short, is a pale, clear lager with a refreshing hoppy taste. It's the perfect tipple for hot summer days.

Weizen, or Weissbier, is a smooth, tangy, slightly sweetish wheat beer that is gold to amber in colour. Choose between Kristallweizen (clear and filtered) and Hefeweizen (cloudy and unfiltered).

Helles A light gold, malty larger that is well balanced and has a crisp, clean finish.

Dunkles, or Dunkel, refers to a dark beer ranging from mahogany to deep brown in hue. It has a distinct malty aroma and can be lightly or heavily hopped.

Berliner Weisse, a specialty of Berlin, is a tangy, top-fermented wheat beer, often with a *Schuss* (dash) of woodruff or raspberry syrup and served in a goblet-style glass.

---

big on the menu with favorites such as salted ribs, knuckles, and sausage salad. *Spreeufer 4.* ☎ *030-24-24-24-4. www.georgbraeu.de. Mon–Fri 12pm–late, Sat-Sun 10am–late. S-Bahn: Alexanderplatz.*

⓫ ★ Microbrauerei Barkowsky. This cozy, unpretentious microbrewery attracts a loyal following. Homebrewed pilsners and ales are available by the glass, meter, or in 5-liter kegs that you can tap yourself. Or try the homemade coffee, and herb and beer liqueurs. Mop up the beer with hearty food like pork knuckles and bratwurst with lashings of sauerkraut. *Münzstrasse 1–3.* ☎ *030-247-69-85. www. brau-dein-bier.de. Daily noon to 1am. U-Bahn: Weinmeisterstrasse.*

⓬ ★ Berliner-Kindl-Schultheiss-Brewery. Little has changed at Berlin's most famous brewery since Jobst Schultheiss founded it in 1853. It still brews classic tipples such as Berliner Pilsner, Kindl, and spicy Schultheiss. Call ahead to join a

1½ hour tour (available in English) to taste the beer and take a behind-the-scenes look at the different brewing processes. *Indira-Gandhi-Strasse 66–69.* ☎ *030-960-90. 5€ tour, 7€–9€ with tasting. Tours Mon–Thurs 10am, 2pm, and 5:30pm. S-Bahn: Landsberger Allee.*

⓭ ★★ kids Prater. Bang in the heart of up-and-coming Prenzlauer Berg, the lively Prater beer garden has a brewing tradition stretching back to 1837. There's nothing better on a hot day than pulling up a bench under the chestnut trees to slurp draught Prater Pils (light lager) or *Schwarzbier* (dark beer). People from all walks of life gather to drink, chomp on Bavarian-style white sausages with sweet mustard, and watch the world go by. The vibe is relaxed and there's even a playground for kids to let off steam. *Kastanienallee 7–9.* ☎ *030-448-56-88. www.pratergarten.de. Oct–Mar Mon–Sat 6pm–late, Sun noon–late; Apr–Sept daily noon–late. U-Bahn: Eberswalder Strasse.*

Kinder Surprise

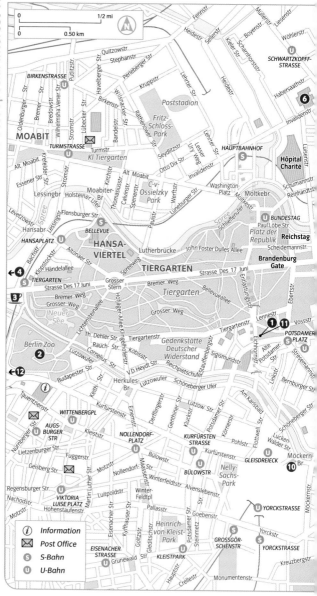

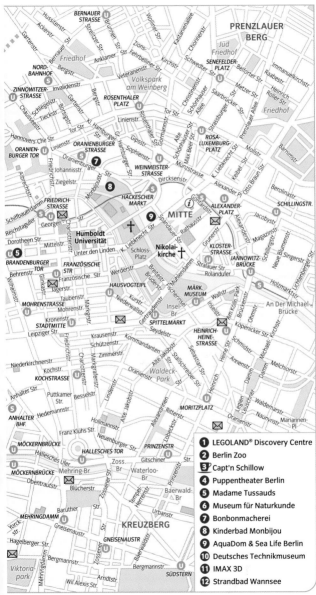

1 LEGOLAND® Discovery Centre
2 Berlin Zoo
3 Capt'n Schillow
4 Puppentheater Berlin
5 Madame Tussauds
6 Museum für Naturkunde
7 Bonbonmacherei
8 Kinderbad Monbijou
9 AquaDom & Sea Life Berlin
10 Deutsches Technikmuseum
11 IMAX 3D
12 Strandbad Wannsee

Berlin is tailor-made for tots, with animal encounters at the zoo, picnics in Tiergarten, seeing the world's biggest Brachiosaurus or a visit to Wannsee to build sandcastles on the beach. Even simple things will spark little imaginations, from munching sausages at a roadside stall to riding in a double-decker bus. START: **U-Bahn to Potsdamer Platz.**

① ★ kids **LEGOLAND® Discovery Centre.** A 7m (23 ft.) giraffe, built from 375,000 Lego bricks, greets you at this interactive attraction inside the Sony Center. Younger children will have a whale of a time getting creative building skyscrapers or racing cars. Big draws include the Lego Studios, where Marilyn Monroe makes an appearance, and Miniland Berlin, where kids can pick out models of the city's famous landmarks such as the 3,000-brick Berliner Dom. ⏱ *1 hr. Sony Center.* ☎ *030-301-04-00. www.legolanddiscoverycentre.de. Admission 15.95€ adults, 13.95€ children under 11. Daily 10am–7pm. U-Bahn: Potsdamer Platz.*

② ★★★ kids **Berlin Zoo.** Set in the expansive greenery of Tiergarten, the spacious, animal-friendly enclosures at this zoo are exemplary. Discover zebras, elephants, pelicans, alpacas, hippos, and the resident giant panda. Make the most of your trip to the zoo by scheduling one of

A pink flamingo enjoys the shade at Berlin Zoo.

these feeding times: Polar bears and seals (10:30am); giant panda (11:30am and 3pm); monkeys (noon and 4pm); penguins (1:45pm); hippos (2:45pm); pelicans (3:30pm). ⏱ *1½ hr. Hardenbergplatz 8.* ☎ *030-25-40-10. www.zoo-berlin.de. Admission*

The mirror image of the giraffe outside LEGOLAND® Discovery Centre.

13€ adults, 10€ concessions, 6.50€ children under 15. Mid-Mar–early Oct daily 9am–7pm; early Oct–mid-Mar 9am–5pm. S-Bahn: Zoologischer Garten.

3 Capt'n Schillow. The kids will love this houseboat moored on the Landwehrkanal. Take a seat on the deck at lunchtime and enjoy a fishy meal of marinated herring with roast potatoes. The houseboat is easy to miss: From Charlottenburger Tor follow a narrow tree-fringed path to Lichtensteinbrücke. Strasse des 17 Juni. ☎ 030-31-50-50-15. €–€€.

4 kids Puppentheater Berlin. The traditional puppets and marionettes that play to crowds at this small theater near Schloss Charlottenburg captivate kids. Performances ranging from Noah's Ark to classic German fairytales such as Hansel and Gretel are bound to put a smile on their faces. The talented puppeteers often encourage children to take part in hands-on activities after the show. Full program details are published on the website. ⏱ 1 hr. Gierkeplatz 2. ☎ 030-342-19-50. www.puppentheater-berlin.de. Tickets 6€–14€. S-Bahn: Westend.

5 ★★ kids Madame Tussauds. Kids will be amazed by the lifelike waxworks at this new Madame Tussauds. Take them to see Shrek, the loveable ogre, and pop stars like Britney Spears and Lady Gaga. See p 80.

6 ★★ kids Museum für Naturkunde. What's 150 million years old, as tall as a four-story building, and as heavy as 10 elephants? Answer: the world's largest Brachiosaurus skeleton at Berlin's Natural History Museum. It's

amazing to see kids wide-eyed as they catch their first glimpse of the prehistoric giant (13m tall and 15.5m long) in the central hall. Although dino may be the star of the show, the rest of the collection is also impressive, spanning everything from fossilized sea urchins to minerals and meteorites. Intriguing creatures on display include the pudú (the world's smallest deer), the musk ox, and the elusive Kirk's dik-dik. Keep an eye out for the jaws of a great white shark near the exit. ⏱ 1 hr. Invalidenstrasse 43. ☎ 030-20-93-85-91. www.naturkunde museum-berlin.de. Admission 5€ adults, 3€ children under 16. Tues–Fri 9:30am–6pm, Sat–Sun 10am–6pm. U-Bahn: Zinnowitzer Strasse.

7 ★ kids Bonbonmacherei. Entering this old-fashioned sweet shop in the Heckmann Höfe is like stepping onto the film set for Charlie and the Chocolate Factory. There's no Willy Wonka, but there is a candy man and kids love to watch him make bonbons by hand in the show kitchen. Whiffs of licorice and peppermint fill the air; scoop yourselves hardboiled sweets from zesty lime drops and raspberry bonbons

Marionettes perform at Puppentheater Berlin.

Playtime in Berlin

With the gigantic Tiergarten (p 96) at its heart, Berlin is one of Europe's greenest cities. It's also dotted with adventure playgrounds where tots can burn off excess energy. One of the most central is the play area on **John-Foster-Dulles-Allee** near the Haus der Kulturen der Welt, with tire swings, ropes, and a sandpit. Edging farther east you reach the **Volkspark** in Friedrichshain with equipment including a pirate ship, a lighthouse, water pumps, and wobbly bridges. Another top choice is **Lausitzer Platz** close to Görlitzer Bahnhof, where children can have fun squirting water and digging in the sand. See map p 96.

to leaf-shaped *Maiblätter* (May leaves), made with woodruff. Spin the signs to find their names in English and German. ⏱ *15 min. Heckmann Höfe.* ☎ *030-44-05-52-43. www.bonbonmacherei.de. Wed–Sat noon–8pm, closed Sun–Tues. S-Bahn: Oranienburger Strasse.*

8 kids **Kinderbad Monbijou.** On balmy summer days, take your children to this family-friendly lido. While grownups relax on the lawns, kids can splash in the shallow pools or test out the whizzy slides. Kinderbad Monbijou is among the most

Sample hard-boiled sweets made the old-fashioned way at Bonbonmacherei.

central of Berlin's public outdoor pools, but for a complete list check the website. *Oranienburger Strasse 78.* ☎ *030-282-86-52. www.berliner baederbetriebe.de. Admission 4€ adults, 2.50€ concessions, 7€ family. Mid-May–June Mon–Fri 11am–7pm, Sat–Sun 10am–7pm; July–Aug daily 10am–7pm. S-Bahn: Oranienburger Strasse.*

9 kids **AquaDom & Sea Life Berlin.** Discover answers to the mystery of the ocean and trace Berlin's waterways from the River Spree to Wannsee at this marine center. Rays and hound sharks glide past in the tanks, and tots can handle starfish in the touch pools. A highlight is the Giant Pacific Octopus, the master of camouflage with a 2m (6½ ft.) arm span. An elevator whisks you through the 25m (82 ft.) AquaDom, the world's largest freestanding aquarium. Get here early to beat the queues. ⏱ *1 hr. Spandauer Strasse 3.* ☎ *030-99-28-00. www.sealife europe.com. Admission 16.95€ adults, 11.95€ children under 14. Daily 10am–7pm. S-Bahn: Hackescher Markt.*

10 ★★ kids **Deutsches Technikmuseum.** Discover the technical wizardry of the past and future at this cavernous museum in

Kreuzberg. The entrance is crowned by a DC-3 plane, nicknamed the "candy bomber" during the 1948–49 **Berlin Airlift** (p 52), because pilots threw gum and chocolate to children below. Kids can peek into the compartments of early-20th-century steam trains, marvel at bizarre homemade flying contraptions, and wander the gardens to glimpse Dutch windmills. At the adjacent Spectrum science center hands-on exhibits are arranged thematically from optical illusions to flow dynamics. ⏱ *1 hr. Trebbiner Strasse 9.* ☎ *030-90-25-40. www.dtmb.de. Admission 4.50€ adults, 2.50€ concessions. Tues–Fri 9am–5:30pm, Sat–Sun 10am–6pm. U-Bahn: Möckernbrücke.*

The Dutch windmill in the gardens at Deutsches Technikmuseum.

⑪ kids IMAX 3D. Entertain kids after dark with a trip to the world's biggest 3D cinema, forming part of the **Sony Center** (p 89) on Potsdamer Platz. The mammoth cinema screens blockbusters and animated films: From underwater voyages to dinosaur encounters. Slip on your special 3D glasses and the effects on the screen become incredibly lifelike. It is advisable to book ahead. *Potsdamer Strasse 4.*

☎ *030-26-06-64-00. www.cinestar-imax.de. Tickets 10€ adults, 8€ children under 12. U-Bahn: Potsdamer Platz.*

⑫ ★★ kids Strandbad Wannsee. In the height of summer, nothing beats a day spent building sandcastles, splashing in the lake, and running free at Wannsee. Don't forget to pack a bucket and spade. *See p 100.*

Kinder Cafes

At Berlin's family-oriented Kinder cafes, moms and dads can take time out while the little ones enjoy free play. The concept is simple but clever: A relaxed cafe vibe and homemade cake or snacks for grownups, a safe play area for tots, and climbing frames, ball pits, puppets, and toys for older kids. Most Kinder cafes are open daily from 10am to 6:30 or 7pm and charge a nominal entrance fee of around 2€ for children. My favorites include **Das Spielzimmer** (Schliemannstrasse 37; 030-44-03-76-35; www.das-spielzimmer.net) in Prenzlauer Berg, and **Kinderwirtschaft** (Schreinerstrasse 15; 030-42-02-52-59; www.kinder-wirtschaft.de) and **Die Knilchbar** (Krossener Strasse 8; 030-29-36-79-89; www.knilchbar.de) in Friedrichshain.

Dark Past, Bright Future

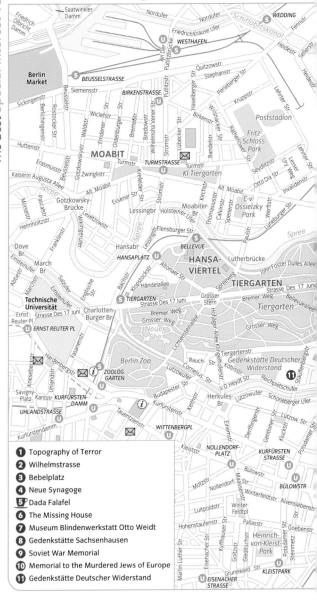

1. Topography of Terror
2. Wilhelmstrasse
3. Bebelplatz
4. Neue Synagoge
5. Dada Falafel
6. The Missing House
7. Museum Blindenwerkstatt Otto Weidt
8. Gedenkstätte Sachsenhausen
9. Soviet War Memorial
10. Memorial to the Murdered Jews of Europe
11. Gedenkstätte Deutscher Widerstand

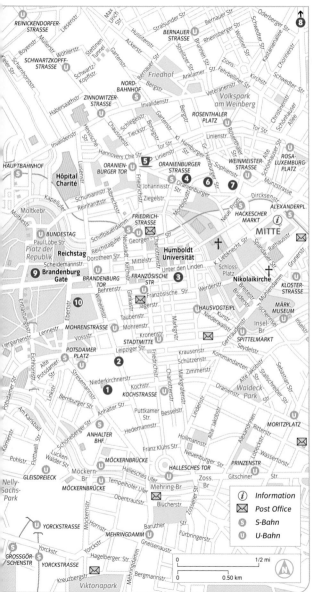

To really understand Berlin, you need to revisit its past; this tour visits Wilhelmstrasse, where the Nazis rose to power in 1933, the Topography of Terror, documenting their monstrous crimes, and memorials commemorating victims of the Holocaust. It looks at how Berlin has rebuilt itself to become the open-minded and innovative capital it is today. START: **S-Bahn to Anhalter Bahnhof.**

❶ ★★★ Topography of Terror. This exhibition chronicling National Socialism (1933–45) and the darkest period of German history chills me to the bone every time. The modern building sits on the site that was once the Gestapo (Secret State Police) headquarters, where the Nazi regime planned and executed atrocities. Information panels and eyewitness accounts are displayed along a walkable timeline tracing Adolf Hitler's jubilant rise to power on January 30, 1933, to the harrowing stories of torture and public humiliation and the post-war trials of SS officers. The photos are too graphic for children. ⏱ *1 hr. Niederkirchnerstrasse 8.* ☎ *030-25-45-09-50. www.topographie.de. Admission free. Daily 10am–8pm. S-Bahn: Anhalter Bahnhof.*

The Topography of Terror documents the horrific crimes of the Holocaust.

❷ Wilhelmstrasse. You're now at the epicenter of Nazi control during the Third Reich. Wilhelmstrasse is where Hitler stripped away the trees for his favorite architect Albert Speer to build a bombastic Reich Chancellery in 1938, complete with a balcony to greet the cheering masses. It was the political stage for parades and marches, and the location of Joseph Goebbels's hateful Propaganda Ministry. Mercifully little remains today; the buildings that weren't bombed in World War II were later demolished. All, that is, with the glaring exception of the austere Reich Air Ministry on the corner of Leipziger Strasse, which now houses the German Finance Ministry. ⏱ *30 min. Wilhelmstrasse. S-Bahn: Anhalter Bahnhof.*

❸ ★ Bebelplatz. Be sure to glance down when crossing this cobbled square opposite the **Humboldt University** (p 41), because it's easy to miss the centerpiece: Micha Ullmann's 1995 *versunkene Bibliothek* (sunken library). Peer through the glass panel to view the stark white walls lined with rows of empty bookshelves. The emotive memorial marks the spot where the first Nazi book burning took place on May 10, 1933 (p 82). A total of 20,000 literary works, including titles by Heinrich Heine and Karl Marx, were set alight; these shelves have space for each and every one of them. ⏱ *30 min. Bebelplatz. U-Bahn: Französische Strasse.*

❹ ★★ Neue Synagoge. Gazing up to admire the pristine gold-ribbed

A wrought iron sign marks Bebelplatz just off Unter den Linden.

cupola of this synagogue, it's hard to imagine that this building was set ablaze by the Nazis on *Kristallnacht* (p 174) in 1938, and then heavily bombed in World War II. With its Moorish-inspired curves and terracotta hue, it has risen from the rubble of the Third Reich and been lovingly restored to its original state. Today, it's once again the focal point of the arty Scheunenviertel, Berlin's Jewish quarter. 🕐 *30 min. See p 12.*

5 ★ **Dada Falafel.** This hole-in-the-wall joint serves by far the best falafel in Berlin. Hear the oil sizzle and smell the fresh mint as your food is prepared in front of you. Other tasty snacks include hummus, couscous, and halloumi. For a taste of everything, order the Dada plate. *Linienstrasse 132.* 📞 *017-95-10-54-35.* €.

6 **The Missing House.** As you walk along Grosse Hamburger Strasse, look for French artist and sculptor Christian Boltanski's *Missing House* (1990) opposite the Jewish School. In 1945, a bomb wrecked the neobaroque townhouse that once stood on this spot. Boltanski discovered that the residents were Jewish and dedicated an

installation and memorial to their absence. It consists of a series of plaques marking roughly where the residents lived with their names and occupations. Born to a Jewish father, the artist spent his early childhood hiding from the Nazis; death and disappearance are recurring themes in his work. 🕐 *10 min. Grosser Hamburger Strasse. S-Bahn: Oranienburger Strasse.*

7 ★ **Museum Blindenwerkstatt Otto Weidt.** Tucked down an alley amid crumbling redbrick houses lies this museum dedicated to unsung hero Otto Weidt (1883–1947). In the early 1940s, Weidt set up a workshop to manufacture brooms and brushes, considered vital for military purposes. He employed 30 blind, deaf, and dumb Jews. From 1941 to 1943, he fought to protect his workers from deportation to concentration camps by hiding them behind the business, providing false papers and bribing Gestapo officials. 🕐 *45 min. Rosenthaler Strasse 39.* 📞 *030-28-59-94-07. www.museum-blindenwerkstatt. de. Admission free. Daily 10am–8pm. U-Bahn: Weinmeisterstrasse.*

Head to Dada Falafel for Berlin's tastiest falafel.

Going Underground

What lies above ground in Berlin is only half the story. There's also a subterranean world of hidden air-raid shelters, tunnels, and arms factories. For a sense of what it was like to live here in World War II, join one of the guided **Berliner Unterwelten** (☎ 030-49-91-05-17; http://berlinerunterwelten.de) tours and explore the labyrinth of bunkers that provided shelter when Allied bombers appeared overhead. Tours lasting roughly 90 minutes and costing 10€ for adults and 6€ for children (free for under-7s) depart from Brunnenstrasse at 11am from Wednesday to Sunday and 11am and 1pm on Monday.

⑧ ★★ Gedenkstätte Sachsenhausen. A 45-minute S-Bahn ride from Friedrichstrasse station is the former Sachsenhausen concentration camp, a chilling reminder of Nazi genocide. From 1936 to 1945, some 200,000 people were imprisoned here; tens of thousands died through forced labor and illness, or were tortured or executed. An *Arbeit macht frei* (work sets you free) sign hangs on the gate to what is now a memorial and museum. ⏱ *1½ hr. Strasse der Nationen 22.*

Berlin's Soviet War Memorial pays tribute to soldiers who died fighting the Nazis.

☎ *033-01-20-00. Admission free. Mid-Mar–mid-Oct 8:30am–6pm; mid-Oct-mid-Mar 8:30am–4:30pm. S-Bahn: Oranienburg.*

⑨ ★ Soviet War Memorial. This memorial looms large on Strasse des 17 Juni, flanked as it is by the greenery of Tiergarten. It pays homage to the 20,000 soldiers of the Soviet Armed Forces who died fighting the Nazis in the bloody Battle of Berlin in 1945, when they seized control of the city. Hitler committed suicide in his bunker on April 30 before the battle ended; this memorial was partly built with marble from his Reich Chancellery. There's a sense of might about the stoa (a colonnade), whose central column is topped with a Red Army soldier immortalized in bronze. Note the T-34 tanks and gold plaques emblazoned with the Communist hammer-and-sickle motif, symbolizing the unity between the working class proletariat (hammer) and the peasant (sickle). ⏱ *20 min. Strasse des 17 Juni. S-Bahn: Unter den Linden.*

⑩ ★★ Memorial to the Murdered Jews of Europe. American architect Peter Eisenman's powerful 2005 Monument to the Murdered Jews of Europe is an undulating maze of 2,700 gray

A field of gray stelae at Peter Eisenman's labyrinthine Holocaust Memorial.

concrete *stelae* that can be entered at any point. The irregular slabs become higher as you approach the center, where they almost block out the sun. Below the wave-like monument lies the **Ort der Information** (Information Center), featuring a permanent exhibition dedicated to the victims of the Holocaust. ⏱ *30 min. See p 7.*

⓫ ★ **Gedenkstätte Deutscher Widerstand.** Seek out this quiet courtyard to learn about the German citizens who risked (and often lost) their lives trying to overthrow the Nazi dictatorship. A quiet spot for contemplation, the memorial commemorates the brave individuals of the anti-Nazi resistance. Among them was Claus von Stauffenberg, who failed in his attempt to assassinate Hitler with a bomb on July 20, 1944. The exhibition offers an insight into the lives of the people who had the courage to stand up and speak out against what they knew to be wrong. ⏱ *45 min. Stauffenbergstrasse 13–14.* ☎ *030-26-99-50-00. Admission free. Mon–Fri 9am–6pm, Thurs until 8pm, Sat–Sun 10am–6pm. U-Bahn: Kurfürsten-strasse.*

Stumbling Blocks

Wandering the city, you're almost certain to stumble across one or two *Stolpersteine*. That was the intention of Gunter Demnig, the Cologne artist behind the brass cobblestone plaques that commemorate the victims of National Socialism. Measuring 10cm (4 in.) by 10cm (4 in.), the paving stones mark where victims once lived, and are engraved with their names and fates. It's a simple yet effective

Keep an eye out for the Stolpersteine, commemorating victims of National Socialism.

way of keeping their memories alive. Look out for some of Berlin's 1,400 "stumbling blocks" along Kantstrasse, Oranienstrasse, and Kurfürstendamm.

Art Uncovered

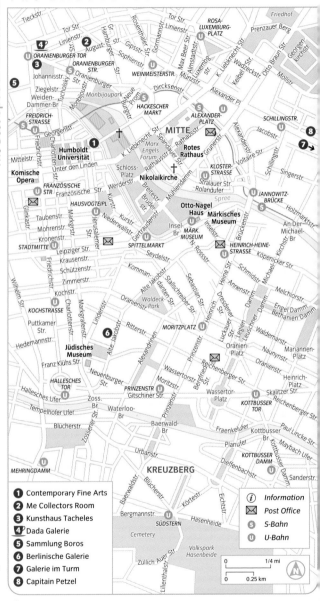

1 Contemporary Fine Arts
2 Me Collectors Room
3 Kunsthaus Tacheles
4 Dada Galerie
5 Sammlung Boros
6 Berlinische Galerie
7 Galerie im Turm
8 Capitain Petzel

(i)	Information
✉	Post Office
S	S-Bahn
U	U-Bahn

B erlin is home to a dynamic and progressive art scene. This tour goes beyond the canvas and takes you to artist-run studios, cafe-bars exhibiting the work of Berlin-based artists, and unique galleries—from a Soviet-era tower block to a World War II bunker. Plug into Berlin's urban culture at squat-turned-arts center Kunsthaus Tacheles and check out Blu's street art in Kreuzberg.
START: S-Bahn to Hackescher Markt.

❶ ★ Contemporary Fine Arts.

Occupying a striking cubic building designed by British architect David Chipperfield, this brilliantly curated gallery sits directly opposite **Museum Island** (p 66). The spotlight has previously focused on high-profile artists such as the German post-modernist painter Georg Baselitz and controversial New York art icon Dash Snow (1981–2009). 🕐 *45 min. Am Kupfergraben 10.* ☎ *030-288-78-70. www.cfa-berlin.com. Admission free. Tues–Fri 11am–6pm, Sat 11am–4pm, closed Sun–Mon. S-Bahn: Hackescher Markt.*

Me Collectors Room.

❷ ★★ Me Collectors Room.

A space for discussing and appreciating art in the widest possible sense is behind collector Thomas

Olbricht's vision. In May 2010, he opened this light, open-plan gallery to show his first-rate contemporary

Scheunenviertel Galleries

This arty neighborhood has a host of innovative and independent galleries, exhibiting (and often selling) contemporary artworks. **Eigen + Art** (Auguststrasse 26; http://cgi.eigen-art.com) houses diverse works by emerging and established creatives, placing the accent on East German art. Berlin-based international artists are in the limelight at the experimental and interactive **DNA Galerie** (Auguststrasse 20; www.dna-galerie.de). Another favorite of mine is the artist-run **Pool Gallery** (Tucholskystrasse 38; www.pool-gallery.com), where up-and-coming artists capture the spirit of the zeitgeist with trans-disciplinary contemporary art. **Berlin Art Projects** (Auguststrasse 50; www.berlinartprojects.de) spotlights emerging Berlin-based artists. Abnormal is predictably the watchword at **Abnormals Gallery** (Linienstrasse 154; http://berlin.abnormalsgallery.com), exploring social issues through art. Bear in mind that most galleries are closed on Monday.

art collection, which features big names like Gerhard Richter as well as emerging talent such as Ouyang Chun, in alternating exhibitions. Upstairs, the *Wunderkammer* spotlights Renaissance and baroque curiosities, from anatomical models to the tusk of a narwhal. See the website for details on events from kids' tours to recitals, talks, and tea ceremonies. ⏱ *1 hr. Auguststrasse 68.* ☎ *030-86-00-85-10. www.me-berlin. com. Admission 6€ adults, 4€ concessions. U-Bahn: Rosenthaler Platz.*

❸ ★★ Kunsthaus Tacheles. Formerly a department store, this dilapidated, graffiti-covered arts center is a post-Wall icon of alternative and street art. Get lost in the labyrinth of ramshackle, paint-sprayed rooms, workshops and studios where you can meet Berlin-based artists and buy their work, plus cafes, performing art spaces, and a courtyard beer garden. On the ground floor is the anticonformist street art academy of Tacheles legend Txus Parras, who has been a fixture at Tacheles since 1992. You can see some of the bold works on display; many are made with recycled objects and spotlight themes like anti-capitalism and global warming. ⏱ *45 min. Oranienburger Strasse 54–56a.* ☎ *030-282-61-85. www.tacheles.de. Admission free. Daily (no fixed times). U-Bahn: Oranienburger Tor.*

❹ ★ Dada Galerie. This high-ceilinged, candlelit gallery-cafe occupies a stylishly converted 19th-century theater. Contemplate the work of up-and-coming artists over drinks or snacks from Dada Falafel (p 33) next door. *Linienstrasse 132.* ☎ *030-27-59-69-27. €.*

❺ ★ Sammlung Boros. Housed in a World War II bunker, Christian Boros's outstanding private collection, opened to the public in 2008,

is perhaps Berlin's most unique. Contemporary works from his collection are shown in rotating exhibitions that emphasize the unusual space; many are installed and staged by the artists themselves. British artist Mark Leckey (Turner Prize winner, 2008) is just one of the 21 artists represented. It's advisable to reserve tickets at least a month in advance if you plan to join one of the 1½ hour art and history tours. ⏱ *1½ hr. Reinhardtstrasse 20.* ☎ *030-27-59-40-65. www.sammlung-boros.de. Admission 10€. Tours in English Fri–Sun 11:30am, 1:30 & 3:30pm; advance reservations essential. U-Bahn: Oranienburger Tor.*

❻ ★★★ Berlinische Galerie. One of Berlin's foremost collections of homegrown fine art, graphic art, photography, and architecture from 1870 to the present day. Temporary exhibitions of contemporary art complement the permanent collection, which zooms in on the Berlin Secession (Max Liebermann and Lovis Corinth), New Objectivity and Expressionism (Otto Dix and George Grosz), Dada (Hannah Höch), and New Figuration of the 1960s (Georg Baselitz). In the forecourt, you can't miss Kühn Malvezzi's *The Glass Warehouse Marker* (2004), a field of enormous shimmering yellow letters listing the major artists represented at the gallery. ⏱ *1 hr. Alte Jakobstrasse 124–128.* ☎ *030-78-90-26-00. www.berlinischegalerie.de. Admission 6€ adults, 4€ concessions. Wed–Mon 10am–6pm. U-Bahn: Hallesches Tor.*

❼ Galerie im Turm. The bombastic Soviet-era Frankfurtur Tor is the backdrop for this gallery, founded by a group of visual artists in 1965. Today the gallery hosts up to 10 exhibitions every year of contemporary painting, drawing, sculpture, print,

Blu is the Color

Ever since the Wall fell, Berlin has embraced street art from the vibrant sprayed murals of the **East Side Gallery** (p 56) to graffiti works on breeze-block apartments in Kreuzberg, Prenzlauer Berg, and Friedrichshain. Italian street art maverick **Blu** has transformed the face of the city with his gigantic, attention-grabbing murals. Step out of Schlesisches Tor U-Bahn station and you'll be confronted by **Back Jump 2007,** an otherworldly figure that seethes with miniature men. Nearby, on the corner of Schlesische Strasse and Curvystrasse is an enormous mural of a headless businessman handcuffed by his wristwatches. Right next to it is **Planet Prozess,** showing two alien-like caricatures. While you're in the neighborhood, check out American artist Jonathan Borofsky's **Molecule Man** (2009), symbolizing the former meeting point of Kreuzberg, Treptow, and Friedrichshain neighborhoods.

Berlin embraces street art.

and installation. There's a strong emphasis on work by Berlin artists. 🕙 *30 min. Frankfurter Tor 1.* ☎ *030-422-94-26. www.kunstamtkreuzberg. de/k_galerieimturm. Admission free. Tues–Sun 2pm–8pm. U-Bahn: Frankfurter Tor.*

8 ★★ **Capitain Petzel.** A remnant of the Soviet era, this glass-clad modernist building is a fitting setting for the gallery opened by Gisela Capitain and Friedrich Petzel in late 2008. Exhibitions home in on works by established artists, such as Americans Kelley Walker, Wade Guyton, and Stephen Prina. 🕙 *45 min. Karl-Marx-Allee 45.* ☎ *030-24-08-81-30. www.capitainpetzel.de. Admission free. Tues–Sat 11am–6pm. U-Bahn: Frankfurter Tor.*

Roaring Twenties

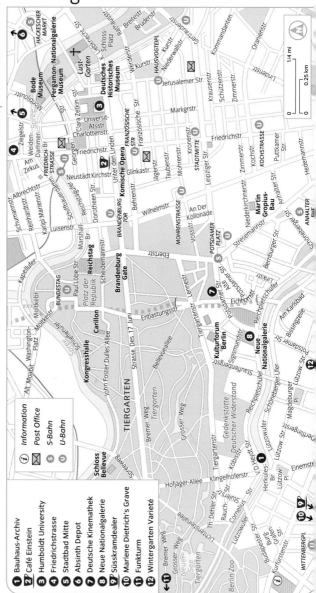

Legend

- (i) Information
- ⊠ Post Office
- S S-Bahn
- U U-Bahn

1. Bauhaus-Archiv
2. Café Einstein
3. Humboldt University
4. Friedrichstrasse
5. Stadtbad Mitte
6. Absinth Depot
7. Deutsche Kinemathek
8. Neue Nationalgalerie
9. Süsskramdealer
10. Marlene Dietrich's Grave
11. Funkturm
12. Wintergarten Varieté

In the 1920s Berlin was a hotbed of hedonism amid the political turmoil of the Weimar Republic; Marlene Dietrich smoldered on stage, the Bauhaus pioneers revolutionized urban design, and artist Otto Dix epitomized New Objectivity with his satirical art. So put your glad rags on and dance the Charleston until dawn on this decadent tour of 1920s Berlin. START: **U-Bahn to Nollendorfplatz.**

1 ★★ **Bauhaus-Archiv.** Like a wave caught in mid-swell, this edifice is based on the design principles of Berlin-born architect and Bauhaus founder Walter Gropius (1883–1969), who believed that "the ultimate aim of all creative activity is a building." From 1919 to 1933, Bauhaus revolutionized design with the aesthetic premise that form meets function, revealing simplicity, clean lines, and the economic utilization of space. Masters such as Russian painter Wassily Kandinsky (1866–1944) and Swiss artist Paul Klee (1879–1940) created their own design vernacular. Step inside to view their floor plans of prefab housing estates, prints, and models, as well as applied arts from tubular steel chairs to ceramics. ⏱ *1 hr. Klingelhöferstrasse 14.* ☎ *030-254-00-20. www.bauhaus. de. Admission 7€ adults, 4€ students, free for children under 11. Wed–Mon 10am–5pm, Tues closed. U-Bahn: Nollendorfplatz.*

Function meets design at the iconic Bauhaus-Archiv.

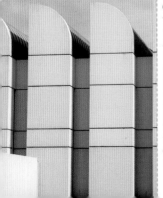

Roam the second-hand book market in front of Berlin's Humboldt University.

2 **Café Einstein.** The aroma of freshly roasted coffee wafts from this bustling 1920s-style cafe. The terrace is a great spot to watch the world go by over a drink or a plate of *Tafelspitz* (Austrian boiled beef). *Unter den Linden 42.* ☎ *030-204-36-32. €€.*

3 ★ **Humboldt University.** As you saunter down Unter den Linden, note the Humboldt University where Albert Einstein (1879–1955) hatched revolutionary theories and taught as a professor in the 1920s. Spy the plaque commemorating Max Planck (1858–1947), Nobel Prize winner and founder of quantum theory, on the left wing; he was among the first to recognize and promote the potential of Einstein's ideas. ⏱ *30 min. Unter den Linden. S-Bahn: Unter den Linden.*

④ Friedrichstrasse. Sequins, stars, feather boas—life was indeed a cabaret on Friedrichstrasse in the Roaring Twenties. For a taste of that glitz and glamor, walk the famous vaudeville mile. Although little remains of its showtime heyday, you can still pick out landmark venues such as the glittering **Friedrich-stadtPalast** (p 135), where Marlene Dietrich made her revue stage debut and showgirls have been wowing audiences since the 1920s. ⏱ *45 min. S-Bahn: Friedrichstrasse.*

⑤ ★ Stadtbad Mitte. You can literally plunge into the 1920s at this Art Deco gem of a swimming pool designed by Heinrich Tessenow. Swim laps in the 50m pool under a tiled glass ceiling. ⏱ *1 hr. Gartenstrasse 5.* ☎ *030-880-90. Admission 4€ adults, 2.50€ concessions. Mon & Wed 6:30am–10:30pm, Tues 6:30am–7pm, Thurs 6:30am–2pm, Fri 6:30am–9:30pm, Sat 2–9pm, Sun 10am–6pm. U-Bahn: Rosenthaler Platz.*

⑥ ★ Absinth Depot. Get into the bohemian spirit of 1920s Berlin at this shop-cum-bar, where the bottles gleam like wizards' potions in this absinthe wonderland. Beware, drink more than one glass of the stuff (3€–5€) and you will indeed be away with the green fairies. *See p 90.*

⑦ ★★ kids Deutsche Kinema-thek. Housed inside the Sony Center (p 89), this film museum takes you back to the days of silent movies and screens clips from 1920s classics such as *The Last Laugh* (1924) and Fritz Lang's sci-fi thriller *Metropolis* (1927). The crowning glory is the permanent exhibition on German actress Marlene Dietrich (1901–92), the mirrored rooms are filled with treasures celebrating the diva's life, from black-and-white portraits to film props, ball gowns, and letters (including one from her close friend Ernest Hemingway). ⏱ *1 hr.*

Potsdamer Strasse 2. www.film museum-berlin.de. ☎ *030-300-90-30. Admission 6€ adults, 4.50€ concessions. Tues–Sun 10am–6pm, Thurs 10am–8pm, Mon closed. U-Bahn: Potsdamer Platz.*

⑧ ★★ Neue Nationalgalerie. Traumatized by World War I and ruffled by shaky Weimar Republic politics, artists began to use their canvases as a sociopolitical stage. There's an emphasis on antiwar Dadaism and provocative, harshly satirical New Objectivity. Look out for works by masters of the genre such as Otto Dix, Max Ernst, and George Grosz. Bauhaus is also represented by the intense colors and abstract motifs of Paul Klee and Wassily Kandinsky. ⏱ *1 hr. Potsdamer Strasse 2. See p 61.*

⑨ ★ Süsskramdealer. With its high ceilings and polished mahogany, this cafe-chocolatier in Friedenau has barely changed since it opened in 1906. Today, owner Martin Hesse pours his passion into three specialties: Coffee, candy, and cocoa. *Varziner Strasse 4.* ☎ *030-85-07-77-97. €–€€.*

Cigarettes and chocolate line the shelves at Süsskramdealer.

Pleasure-Seeking Berlin

Nothing says 1920s Berlin like a wildly hedonistic night on the town. The Roaring Twenties were all about drinking, dancing, and dressing up to excess, and that's just what you'll find at **Bohème Sauvage** club nights, held once monthly in a different glamorous Berlin location. Whether diva or dandy, flapper or gigolo—you'll need to dust off your finery for this glittering affair. Charleston lessons, a casino with (fake) inflation money, cigarette girls, and a dance floor swinging to jazz and tango are all part of the fun. You can order tickets online at www.boheme-sauvage.de. If you can't make it, the next best thing is **Clärchens Ballhaus** (p 126), an old-fashioned ballroom with swing nights every Wednesday.

🔟 ★ Marlene Dietrich's Grave. Enter this cemetery in a quiet corner of the Friedenau district and walk to the back to see a marble tombstone on the right that bears the gold inscription: *Hier Steh ich an den Marken meine Tage* (here I stand at the end of my days). Born in Schöneberg in 1901, Marlene, as Berliners affectionately call her, joined Max Reinhardt's troupe as a chorus girl and actress in 1921. Her big break was in 1930 when she starred in *The Blue Angel* as pouting cabaret diva Lola Lola. She died in Paris in 1992, but chose to be buried close to her mother, Josefine von Losch. Next to Marlene's grave is that of German-Australian fashion photographer Helmut Newton (1920–2004), famous for his racy *Playboy* pinups. 🕐 *30 min. Stubenrauchstrasse 43–45. U-Bahn: Bundesplatz.*

⓫ ★★★ kids Funkturm. Rising 150m (492 ft.) above the city, Berlin's radio tower looks like a distant relative of the Eiffel Tower. Imagine how impressive the lattice steel structure must have been when Heinrich Straumer built it in 1926. I like to visit at dusk when the lights bathe the tower gold, and the entire city twinkles below. 🕐 *45 min. Hammarskjöldplatz 1. ☎ 030-30-38-29-96. Admission 4.50€ adults, 2.50€ concessions. Wed 6–11pm, Tues–Sun 11:30am–11pm. U-Bahn: Kaiserdamm.*

⓬ Wintergarten Varieté. Acrobats and stilt walkers, magicians and conjurers—the Wintergarten is Berlin's most flamboyant cabaret hall. The glitzy variety performances are as popular now as they were in the 1920s, when this was Europe's biggest and most modern theater, sporting the first ever revolving stage. Book tickets ahead (stage-level seats are the most expensive). *See p 136.*

The Funkturm (Radio Tower) illuminated by night.

City **Highs**

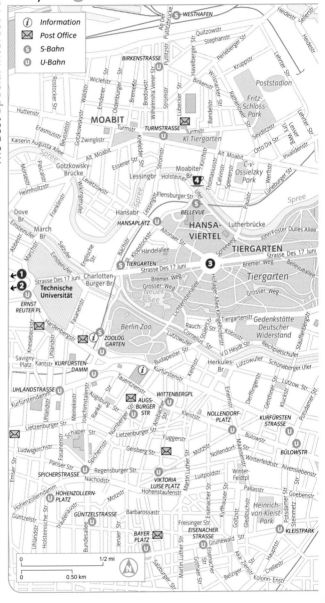

ⓘ	*Information*
✉	*Post Office*
Ⓢ	*S-Bahn*
Ⓤ	*U-Bahn*

Berlin from Above

If the balloon doesn't take you quite high enough, Air Service Berlin (☎ 030-53-21-53-21; www.air-service-berlin.de) also organizes floatplane flights, which take off and land on the River Spree in Treptower Park. A great idea for special occasions, the flights cost 189€ (half price for under-11s) and include a champagne reception. Gliding above Berlin at 600m (1,969 ft.) affords a bird's-eye view of landmarks such as Schloss Charlottenburg, the Funkturm, the Olympic Stadium, and the Brandenburg Gate.

Tiergarten. Be sure to book your tour in advance online. ⏱ *45 min.* *See p 7.*

6 ★ **Französischer Dom.** Rising gracefully above Gendarmenmarkt, this former baroque church is worth a visit for its domed tower, which harbors one of Berlin's biggest *carillons*. Climb 284 steps to the 40m (131 ft.) viewpoint for a great panorama of Mitte, encompassing the Fernsehturm, Berliner Dom, and Rotes Rathaus. ⏱ *30 min. Gendarmenmarkt. www.franzoesischer-dom.de. Admission 2.50€ adults, 1€ children under 14. Daily 10am–7pm. U-Bahn: Französische Strasse.*

7 ★ **Berliner Dom.** You have to earn your views from the Berliner Dom by puffing up 267 steep steps—but it's worth it. Although not one of

Berlin's highest viewpoints, the narrow platform skirting the dome makes it feel like it. Enjoy the sights from your 50m (164 ft.) balcony over the city: From the Lustgarten (p 67) to the Reichstag and Rotes Rathaus (p 64, **7**). ⏱ *45 min.*

8 ★★ **kids Berlin Hi-Flyer.** For a bird's-eye perspective over Berlin, climb into the world's largest tethered balloon. Emblazoned with *Die Welt* ("The World," a German newspaper), the blue-and-white helium giant is visible from almost everywhere in the city. The flight is short (just a few minutes) but spectacular, gently rising above the rooftops to 150m (429 ft.). Here the balloon hovers, so you can stroll around the edge and admire the view stretching from the rainbow-colored GSW

When the sun shines, locals gather at the foot of the mighty Reichstag.

Soar above the city in the Berlin Hi-Flyer, the world's largest tethered balloon.

9 ★★★ kids **Panoramapunkt Potsdamer Platz.** Take a speedy ride on Europe's fastest elevator, whisking you from ground level to 100m (328 ft.) in just 20 seconds. The lift ascends to the 24th and 25th floors of the iconic redbrick Kollhoff-Tower, the highest building in the **Daimler-Chrysler Quartier** (p 61). Up among the skyscrapers, the platform offers a dizzying 360° view of the city's skyline. The tent-like roof of the Sony Center appears incredibly close, and it's possible to spy the Reichstag, Brandenburg Gate, and River Spree. 🕐 *45 min. Potsdamer Platz 1.* ☎ *030-25-29-43-72. www.panoramapunkt. de. Admission 5.50€ adults, 6€ concessions. Daily 10am–6pm; to 8pm Sat. U-Bahn: Potsdamer Platz.*

10 ★ **Panoramacafé.** The floor-to-ceiling windows at this sleek new cafe in the Kollhoff-Tower allow you to enjoy outstanding views over coffee and cake. It's also a terrific spot for a sundowner. *Potsdamer Platz 1.* ☎ *030-25-29-43-72. €.*

11 ★★ kids **Viktoriapark.** Surrounded by lush greenery, the 66m (216 ft.) hill at the heart of Viktoriapark is worth the climb. An easy-to-follow trail shadows the waterfall to the summit, Berlin's highest natural point. Crowning the peak is an 1821 monument commemorating victory in the Napoleonic Wars (1803–15); its cross gives the neighborhood its name (*Kreuzberg* means "cross hill"). Bear in mind, it is not advisable to walk here alone after dark. 🕐 *30 min. Kreuzbergstrasse. Admission free. U-Bahn: Platz der Luftbrücke.*

12 ★ **Oberbaumbrücke.** This bridge is one of my favorite places to watch the sun set. Arrive in the dusky light of late afternoon and you'll see its whimsical redbrick turrets and arches glow. Look along the River Spree to view the silhouette of the Fernsehturm and O2 World and, in the other direction, the **Molecule Man** (p 39). The bridge was originally built in the 18th century and takes its name from the tree trunk used to block the river at night to stop smuggling. It was revamped in 1896 in ornamental Gothic revival style. During the Cold War the bridge was a border crossing between East (Friedrichshain) and West (Kreuzberg) Berlin. 🕐 *20 min. U-Bahn: Schlesisches Tor.*

City view from Panoramapunkt Potsdammer Platz.

⑬ ★★ Fernsehturm. With its iconic wink and silver sphere in orbit, Berlin's tallest building at 368m (1,207 ft.) sneaks into almost every city snapshot. Open until midnight, it's a great choice for a view of Berlin illuminated by night. A lift races to the viewing platform in 40 seconds, from where there is a sweeping view over the city, which extends 40km (25 miles) on a clear day, from the nearby Rotes Rathaus to the Brandenburg Gate, Olympic Stadium, and beyond. When the TV tower was completed in 1969 as a flagship project of the atheist GDR government, the gold cross that appears on the steel globe when sunlight hits it was dubbed the *Rache des Papstes* (the Pope's revenge). ⌚ *45 min. Panoramastrasse 1A.* ☎ *030-242-33-33. www.berlinerfernsehturm.de. Admission 11€ adults, 7€ children under 16. Mar–Oct 9am–midnight; Nov– Feb 10am–midnight. U-Bahn: Alexanderplatz.*

⑭ ★ Solar. Take a lift to the 17th floor to see Berlin unfurl magically before you in this stylish glass-walled lounge. Join a young, good-looking crowd for cocktails and superlative views. *See p 116.* €€€–€€€€.

Solar.

Brick in the Wall

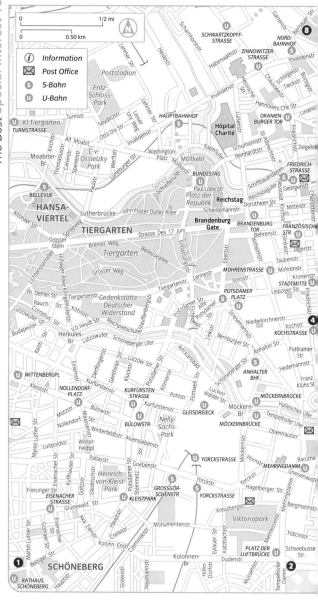

1. Rathaus Schöneberg
2. Tempelhof Luftbrückendenkmal
3. Tempelhofer Park
4. Mauermuseum at Checkpoint Charlie
5. Marx-Engels-Forum
6. DDR Museum
7. Ampelmann
8. Gedenkstätte Berliner Mauer
9. Mauerblümchen
10. Karl-Marx-Allee
11. Café Sibylle
12. Stasi Museum
13. East Side Gallery
14. Ostel

From 1961 to 1989, the Berlin Wall divided the city in two. Visit today and you find that remarkably little remains of this Cold War symbol. From a spin in a Trabant to a night in the Stasi suite, this tour rides the wave of nostalgia which has swept the capital. Tour the monumental Karl-Marx-Allee and relive the greatest escapes at Checkpoint Charlie. **START: U-Bahn to Bayerischer Platz.**

Plaque to John F. Kennedy at Rathaus Schöneberg.

❶ Rathaus Schöneberg. The nondescript facade of Tempelhof-Schöneberg's city hall, dating back to 1914, belies its exceptional history. On June 26, 1963, US president John F. Kennedy gave a speech to express U.S. support for a democratic West Germany: "All free men, wherever they may live, are citizens of Berlin, and, therefore, as a free man, I take pride in the words 'Ich bin ein Berliner'." A bronze plaque pays homage to the former president, who was assassinated in 1964, shortly after the construction of the Wall. Visit the clock tower sheltering the *Freiheitsglocke* (Liberty Bell), which the people of the United States donated to Berlin in 1950; come at midday to hear it chime. ⏱ *1 hr. John-F.-Kennedy-Platz 1. U-Bahn: Bayerischer Platz.*

❷ Tempelhof Luftbrücken-denkmal. Sweeping above Platz der Luftbrücke, this memorial remembers the victims of the Berlin Airlift (1948–49), when Soviets blocked all the major rail and road routes to West Berlin. It was one of the first major crises of the Cold War (1947–91). The only way the Western allies could deliver much-needed supplies was by air. Berliners nickname the memorial the *Hungerkralle* (hunger claw). Once home to military barracks, the pine-fringed square is now a peaceful spot for contemplation. ⏱ *45 min. Platz der Luftbrücke 1. U-Bahn: Platz der Luftbrücke.*

❸ ★★ Tempelhofer Park. Opened in summer 2010 on the site of the former Tempelhof Airport, this 355-hectare (877 acre) open space has become one of Berlin's quirkiest attractions. Indeed, where

The three-pronged Tempelhof Luftbrück-endenkmal commemorating the Berlin Airlift (1948–49).

Go, Trabi, Go!

Take a trip down memory lane behind the wheel of a Trabant (nicknamed "Trabi"), the classic GDR car with a Duroplast body and smoky two-cylinder engine. Back in the not-so-good-old days, folk in East Germany had to wait up to 18 years for one of these slow, unreliable boneshakers. **Trabi Safaris** (☎ 030-27-59-22-73; www. trabi-safari.de) are a fun way to discover Berlin beyond the well-trodden tourist track. A one-hour spin of the "Wild East" whizzes past the East Side Gallery (p 56) and down Karl-Marx-Allee (p 55). Simply book your tour, pick your dream Trabi, and step on the gas—up to 30km/h (18 miles/h)—as a radio guide talks you through the sights. Tours costing 30€–60€ per person depart daily, 10am–6pm, from the corner of Wilhelmstrasse and Zimmerstrasse.

Happy driver behind the wheel a Trabant on a Trabi Safari.

else can you jog and rollerblade along runways and picnic in front of the terminals? When it snows in winter, there are even cross-country ski tracks. Berliners love their new park for its history, novelty value, and wonderful views of the city skyline. ⏱ 45 min. ☎ 030-700-90-60. www. gruen-berlin.de Admission free. Jan & Dec daily 7.30am–5pm; Feb & Nov daily 7am; Mar & Oct daily 6am–7pm; Apr & Sept 6am–8:30pm; May & Aug 6am–9:30pm; June & July daily 6am–10:30pm. S-Bahn: Platz der Luftbrücke.

④ ★ Mauermuseum at Checkpoint Charlie. Opposite the reconstructed guardhouse at Checkpoint Charlie (p 15, ②), this museum traces the rise and fall of the Berlin Wall. Though the museum can be cramped at times, it's still a touching portrayal of once-divided Berlin. Alongside black-and-white photos narrating the history of the Wall are accounts of ingenious escape attempts from East to West Berlin. Ingenuity stretched from shovels for digging tunnels and hidden compartments in VW cars to faux Soviet uniforms and hot-air balloons. ⏱ 45 min. Friedrichstrasse 43–45. ☎ 030-53-72-50. www.mauermuseum.de. Admission 12.50€ adults, 9.50€ concessions. Daily 9am–10pm. U-Bahn: Kochstrasse.

⑤ Marx-Engels-Forum. The officially atheist GDR was not without its iconic figures. These included economist-philosophers Karl Marx (1818–83) and Friedrich Engels (1820–95), the founding fathers of Socialism and authors of the Communist Manifesto (1848), which spearheaded the Communist movement Europe-wide. Immortalized in bronze, the pair loom above this square in former East Berlin. Note

Werner Stötzer's 1985 Bulgarian marble relief wall behind them, depicting people in an early Capitalist society. Get here early for the best light and fewer crowds. ⏱ *30 min. Marx-Engels-Forum. S-Bahn: Alexanderplatz.*

6 ★★★ kids **DDR Museum.** For a hands-on experience of daily life in the German Democratic Republic (GDR), little beats this museum by the River Spree. Laid out like a prefab housing estate, 17 themed rooms transport you back to the former East Germany, which existed from 1949 until 1990. Everything on display can be touched: answer the phone in the Soviet-era living room, rummage through closets, or rev the engine of a Trabant. From typical food brands to the famous FDJ (Free German Youth) shirts, Erika typewriters to table football, the museum takes a fond look at everyday lives of ordinary East Germans. There's even a dedicated exhibition on the classlessness and freedom of *Freikörperkultur* (FKK), or naturism, in the GDR. ⏱ *1 hr. Karl-Liebknecht-Strasse 1.* ☎ *030-847-12-37-31. www.ddr-museum.de. Admission 6€ adults, 4€ concessions. Daily 10am–8pm, Sat until 10pm. S-Bahn Friedrichstrasse.*

Get to the Marx-Engels-Forum early to beat the crowds.

7 **Ampelmann.** Keep an eye out when you cross the road for the beloved traffic-light man, or *Ampelmännchen*, a lasting symbol from the GDR that has now achieved cult status. Threatened with extinction when the Wall crumbled, the little man has survived at most pedestrian crossings. Walk this way for *Ampelmännchen* memorabilia from T-shirts to corkscrews. ⏱ *20 min. See p 92.*

8 ★ **Gedenkstätte Berliner Mauer.** Bernauer Strasse is one of the few places where you can view the Berlin Wall as it really was: crude and unadorned. Commemorating victims of Communist tyranny, this memorial is the only location where you can still see the "death strip," a narrow corridor between the two walls that was booby-trapped and patrolled by guards. It's an ugly sight. Right opposite, the Documentation Center takes an in-depth look at the construction of the Wall with text, photos, and film excerpts. Next door, peek inside the oval-shaped Kapelle der Versöhnung (Chapel of Reconciliation), built from rammed earth and wooden staves, which opened in 2000 to replace a church torn down when the Wall was erected. ⏱ *1 hr. Bernauer Strasse 111.* ☎ *030-467-98-66-66. Admission free. Documentation Center Apr–Oct Tues–Sun 9:30am–7pm; Nov–Mar Tues–Sun 9:30am–6pm; closed Mon. U-Bahn: Bernauer Strasse.*

The iconic Ampelmännchen (traffic-light man) at the DDR Museum.

Milestones in History

Next time you're at the Brandenburg Gate (p 7), Bernauer Strasse (p 54), or Potsdamer Platz (p 11), look down as well as up. You'll notice a double row of red cobblestones, punctuated by metal plaques that bear the inscription: "Berliner Mauer 1961–1989." The Berlin Wall History Mile marks where the Wall once stood, and is a startling flashback to how the divided city must have looked. Thirty information panels complement this line of pavestones, providing some historical background on the Wall, including several accounts of escape attempts.

9 ★ **Mauerblümchen.** Aptly named "wallflower," this no-frills restaurant in Prenzlauer Berg rolls out GDR favorites such as spicy Solyanka (Russian beef and vegetable stew) and Schmalzbrot (bread and dripping) in nostalgic surroundings. *Wisbyer Strasse 4.* ☎ *030-444-79-04.* €.

10 ★★ **Karl-Marx-Allee.** The scale of this monumental East Berlin boulevard is dizzying. Built in the 1950s and named Stalinallee until 1961, it was the showcase for the grand designs of Socialist Realism, and provided the backdrop for Soviet tanks, marching soldiers, and the annual May Day parade. To appreciate its dimensions, walk all the way to the mighty watchtowers of the 1956 Frankfurter Tor gateway. The avenue is lined with eight-story buildings that are as intimidating as they are impressive, erected in the *Zuckerbäckerstil* (wedding-cake style) with soaring lines and ionic pillars. Many scenes in the bittersweet German comedy *Goodbye Lenin* (2003) were filmed here. ⏱ *45 min. Karl-Marx-Allee. U-Bahn: Schillingstrasse or Frankfurter Tor.*

11 **Café Sibylle.** Enjoy coffee and homemade cake or ice cream with a dollop of Cold War charm at this cafe. You can take a break surrounded by GDR posters recounting the history of Karl-Marx-Allee and curios, including a fragment of stone moustache—all that's left of a once mighty Stalin statue. *Karl-Marx-Allee 72.* ☎ *030-29-35-22-03.* €.

12 ★★ **Stasi Museum.** This eerie museum occupies the former headquarters of the East Ministry for State Security, or Stasi (1950–90). It revisits the days when 85,000 Communist secret police gathered intelligence by spying on their own citizens and paying 170,000 informers to record the lives of friends, colleagues, and families. This violation of human rights took place on a vast scale, creating 17 million index cards and files that if laid out end-to-end would stretch 180km (112 miles). The stark rooms display GDR medals, flags, photos, and spying equipment, including cameras and infrared beamers. The exhibition on resistance reveals how thousands of citizens were kidnapped and imprisoned in inhumane conditions. Don't miss the drab office of Erich Mielke, Stasi head from 1957–89, preserved

Wall art at the East Side Gallery — the longest remaining stretch of the Berlin Wall.

in its original state. Pick up an English booklet at the entrance as most information is in German. 🕐 *45 min. Ruschestrasse 103. ☎ 030-553-68-54. www.stasimuseum.de. Admission 4€ adults, 3€ concessions. Mon–Fri 11am–6pm, Sat–Sun 2–6pm. U-Bahn: Magdalenenstrasse.*

⓭ ★★ kids East Side Gallery. Make a beeline for the longest and best-preserved stretch of the Berlin Wall, near Ostbahnhof station. This

Ostel Hotel.

open-air gallery displays over 100 politically charged airbrush works, painted by artists from 21 countries, which gave the concrete a new *raison d'être* in 1990. Recently given a fresh lick of paint, the murals now serve as a memorial to German freedom. One of the most controversial pieces is Dimitrij Vrubel's *Bruderkuss* (Brotherly Kiss), showing former Soviet leader Leonid Brezhnev and East German leader Erich Honecker kissing. 🕐 *45 min. See p 56.*

⓮ ★ Ostel. If you're not already dreaming of the GDR, you will be when you enter this tower block hotel, oozing *Ostalgia* (nostalgia for the former East Germany) from every Soviet pore. A picture of beaming East German official Horst Sindermann (1915–90) graces the reception, where clocks show the time in Moscow, Havana, and Beijing. Snooze under portraits of politicians in a prefab apartment, check into the Stasi suite complete with bugging devices, or bed down in the budget pioneer dorm. *Wriezener Karree 5. ☎ 030-25-76-86-60. www.ostel.eu. Dorm bed 15€, singles 33€, doubles 54€. S-Bahn: Ostbahnhof.* ●

Tiergarten & Potsdamer Platz

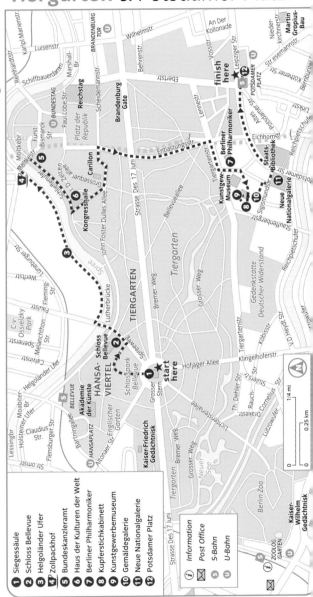

1 Siegessäule
2 Schloss Bellevue
3 Helgoländer Ufer
4 Zollpackhof
5 Bundeskanzleramt
6 Haus der Kulturen der Welt
7 Berliner Philharmoniker
8 Kupferstichkabinett
9 Kunstgewerbemuseum
10 Gemäldegalerie
11 Neue Nationalgalerie
12 Potsdamer Platz

(i) Information
⊠ Post Office
S S-Bahn
U U-Bahn

Previous page: Marx-Engels-Forum.

The his tour leads from the green expanse of **Tiergarten** to a forest of skyscrapers in Potsdamer Platz. Following the River Spree, take in the neoclassical grandeur of Schloss Bellevue and the curvy Haus der Kulturen der Welt. Ambling farther south brings you to Kulturforum's stellar galleries showcasing Rembrandt and Picasso. START: **S-Bahn to Tiergarten.**

Manicured lawns sweep up to Prussian palace Schloss Bellevue.

❶ ★★ **Siegessäule.** One of Berlin's most visible icons, the Siegessäule towers above the Grosser Stern roundabout and is crowned by a golden Victoria statue, nicknamed "Goldene Else" by Berliners. You need to get up close to this monument to Prussian war victories to appreciate its ornate murals and mosaics, depicting the battle of the 19th-century Franco-Prussian and Austro-Prussian wars. Feeling sprightly? Scramble up to the platform for fantastic vistas across the treetops to central Berlin. ⏱ *30 min. See p 13. S-Bahn: Tiergarten.*

❷ **Schloss Bellevue.** Pass through mature woodlands linking Grosser Stern to Schloss Bellevue. Stroll across the neatly clipped lawns to reach the three-winged facade of this beautiful baroque palace. Built in 1786 for Prince Ferdinand of Prussia, it has been the official residence of the German president since 1994. Supported by Corinthian columns, the gables are embellished with allegorical figures that represent agriculture, fishing, and hunting. ⏱ *20 min. See p 13.*

❸ ★ kids **Helgoländer Ufer.** On a sunny day the maple- and willow-fringed banks of the River Spree draw everyone from young couples to joggers and stroller-pushing parents. As tour boats glide past, and landmarks such as the Bundeskanzleramt (❺) and the Haus der Kulturen der Welt (❻) slide into view, I plant myself on one of the benches and soak up the atmosphere. ⏱ *45 min.*

❹ kids **Zollpackhof.** This riverside beer garden overlooking the Bundeskanzleramt is the perfect spot to relax with a cool drink under the chestnut trees. There's also a small playground for kids. *See p 20.* €€.

❺ **Bundeskanzleramt.** Berliners call their Federal Chancellery the *Elefanten-Waschanlage* (elephant washing machine). It's a fitting description for this giant white cube, which houses the office of the German chancellor. Built in 2001 by Berlin architects Axel Schultes and Charlotte Frank, the postmodernist edifice is a striking addition to Berlin's riverfront. Walk around to get a

On Yer Bike!

Walking aside, one of the best ways to explore Berlin is from a bicycle saddle. American-owned **Fat Tire Bike Tours** (☎ 030-24-04-79-91; www.fattirebiketoursberlin.com) offers tours with native English-speaking guides that are suitable for all ages. The 4½ hour All-In-One City Bike Tour (20€ adults, 18€ concessions, 12€ children) is an enjoyable way to see the highlights of Berlin, taking in sights like the Siegessäule (p 13, **⑩**), Checkpoint Charlie (p 15, **②**), and Potsdamer Platz (p 11). Tours depart daily at 11am from the Fernsehturm on Alexanderplatz from March to October; also at 4pm from mid-May to late September. From November to February, there are two tours weekly at 11am on Wednesday and Saturday.

feel for its scale and admire its pillars, ruler-straight lines, and arch of windows. 🕐 *15 min. Willy-Brandt-Strasse 1. S-Bahn: Hauptbahnhof.*

⑥ ★ kids Haus der Kulturen der Welt. A gift from the U.S. government to Berlin in 1957, the cultural venue Berliners nickname the pregnant oyster always has me reaching for my camera. Cross the Spree to get close to its arched roof, dappled with sunlight from the reflection of the Spiegelteich (mirror pond). 🕐 *15 min. See p 12.*

⑦ Berliner Philharmoniker. German architect Hans Scharoun channeled his vision into revamping this corner of Berlin in the 1960s. The honeycombed facade and pointy peaks of his philharmonic hall look like an asymmetrical big top. Classical music fans admire it more for the impressive acoustics, particularly when the resident Berliner Philharmoniker Orchestra, conducted by Brit Sir Simon Rattle, is in the pit. 🕐 *15 min. See p 136.*

⑧ ★ Kupferstichkabinett. This gallery creaks under the weight of its peerless graphic arts collection, which is the largest in Germany. Among its cache of prints, drawings,

pastels, and oils are star pieces by Renaissance painter and engraver Albrecht Dürer (1471–1528), Dutch Golden Age master Rembrandt van Rijn (1606–69), and Florentine Renaissance artist Sandro Botticelli (ca.1444–1510), plus 20th-century masterpieces by Picasso and Warhol. 🕐 *1 hr. Matthäikirchplatz.*

The golden, honeycombed facade of the Berliner Philharmoniker.

☎ *030-266-42-42-01. Admission 3€ adults, 3€ concessions; Kulturforum combined ticket 12€ adults, 6€ concessions. Tues–Fri 10am–6pm, Sat–Sun 11am–6pm. U-Bahn: Potsdamer Platz.*

⑨ Kunstgewerbemuseum.
This treasure-trove of decorative arts shelters everything from Renaissance bronze and Meissen porcelain to delicate Venetian glassware and majolica (glazed earthenware). The diverse collection also encompasses taffeta ball gowns, Chinese ceramics, and hand-crafted glass. Look out for the Merseburger Spiegelkabinett, an 18th-century room carved from linden wood and adorned with gold, ivory, and mirrors.
🕐 *45 min. Herbert-von-Karajan-Strasse 10.*
☎ *030-266-42-43-01. Admission 8€ adults, 4€ concessions; Kulturforum combined ticket 12€ adults, 6€ concessions. Tues–Fri 10am–6pm, Sat–Sun 11am–6pm. U-Bahn: Potsdamer Platz.*

⑩ ★★★ Gemäldegalerie. This is Berlin's must-see picture gallery, particularly for fans of the Old Masters. Anyone with an interest in art will be captivated by works from the brushes of Peter Paul Rubens, Titian, Botticelli, Goya, Andrea Mantegna, and—best of all—Rembrandt van Rijn, whose masterpieces take up a whole room. You need time if you plan to explore all 72 rooms; or pick up a gallery map to pinpoint the highlights. 🕐 *1 hr. See p 11.*

⑪ ★★ Neue Nationalgalerie.
Bringing you back to the 20th century, the New National Gallery hosts a star-studded lineup of contemporary artists. Architect Mies van der Rohe's 1968 glass-and-steel edifice provides the backdrop for recent European painting and sculpture. Cubist works by Pablo Picasso and surrealist pieces by Salvador Dali (1904–89) hang alongside Bauhaus creations by Paul Klee (1879–1940) and his friend, the painter Wassily Kandinsky (1866–1944). Conceived by Berlin architect Walter Gropius in 1919, the ethos of the Bauhaus school was to unite form and function. The school was a galvanic force in Modernist architecture and a staunch opponent of Expressionism. Labeling Bauhaus styles un-German and Communist-inspired, Nazis closed down the school in 1933. 🕐 *1 hr. Potsdamer Strasse 50.* ☎ *030-266-26-51. Admission 8€ adults, 4€ concessions. Tues–Sun 10am–6pm, Thurs until 10pm. U-Bahn: Potsdamer Platz.*

The station entrance on Potsdamer Platz.

⑫ Potsdamer Platz. After immersing yourself in art for the afternoon, head to Berlin's futuristic Potsdamer Platz. The crystalline Sony Center (p 89) looks otherworldly when it glows silver-blue and magenta by night. Equally progressive is the Daimler-Chrysler Quartier, which emerged from the rubble of the Berlin Wall and took shape under acclaimed Italian architect Renzo Piano. It's one of Europe's largest urban development projects. Potsdamer Platz always has a buzz, but it's perfect to be here in the evening when the skyscrapers glitter and Berliners meet for pre-theater drinks. 🕐 *30 min. See p 11.*

Alexanderplatz & Surrounds

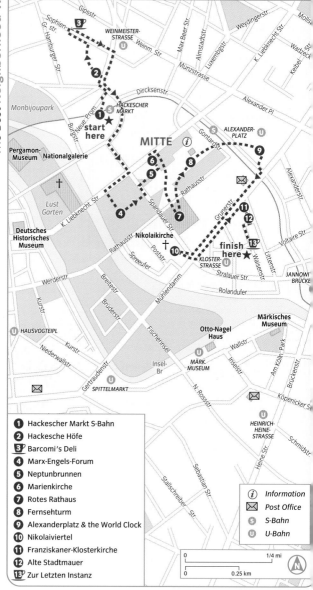

1. Hackescher Markt S-Bahn
2. Hackesche Höfe
3. Barcomi's Deli
4. Marx-Engels-Forum
5. Neptunbrunnen
6. Marienkirche
7. Rotes Rathaus
8. Fernsehturm
9. Alexanderplatz & the World Clock
10. Nikolaiviertel
11. Franziskaner-Klosterkirche
12. Alte Stadtmauer
13. Zur Letzten Instanz

(i) Information
✉ Post Office
Ⓢ S-Bahn
Ⓤ U-Bahn

0		1/4 mi
0	0.25 km	

This tour kicks off at Hackescher Markt, where railway arches harbor boutiques, restaurants, and late-night bars. After seeing the sights of Alexanderplatz, a short walk brings you to the cobbled streets of Nikolaiviertel. Be prepared for a few surprises, including bear encounters in the park and an enchanting Franciscan monastery. START: **S-Bahn to Hackescher Markt.**

❶ Hackescher Markt S-Bahn.
Start your tour at Berlin's loveliest S-Bahn station, built in 1882 at the height of the railway boom. This up-and-coming area is home to bars, restaurants, and boutiques under the arches. It's hard to believe that, until the 19th century, there was nothing here but marshy wasteland. ⏱ *15 min. S-Bahn: Hackescher Markt.*

❷ ★ kids Hackesche Höfe. Edging slightly north, the eight interlinking courtyards of the Hackesche Höfe exude Art Nouveau flair. The prettiest is Hof I, with glazed mosaic walls in myriad shades. Browse the specialist shops for everything from cutting-edge *couture* to Art Deco bangles. Alternatively, unwind on a cafe terrace for espresso and a spot of people-watching. ⏱ *30 min. See p 11.*

❸ ★ kids Barcomi's Deli. Great for lunch, this NYC-style deli is tucked away in a 19th-century courtyard. The bagels, sandwiches with homemade potato or rye bread, wraps, and antipasti are all delicious. Try a freshly roasted coffee with a slice of pecan pie for dessert. *Sophie-Gips-Höfe 2, Sophienstrasse 2.* ☎ *030-28-59-83-63.* €.

❹ Marx-Engels-Forum. Looping back toward Alexanderplatz brings you through this tree-fringed square, where statues of a seated Karl Marx and standing Friedrich Engels form the centerpiece. The larger-than-life fathers of socialism today draw camera-toting tourists

as much as readers of their 1848 *Communist Manifesto.* ⏱ *20 min.*

❺ ★ kids Neptunbrunnen.
Approaching the Fernsehturm, your gaze is drawn to the Neptunbrunnen (Neptune Fountain). The water nymphs at the Roman god's feet are personifying Germany's main rivers: The Elbe, Rhine, and Oder. When the sun's out, kids love to splash in the shallow water on sunny days. ⏱ *15 min. Karl-Liebknecht-Strasse. S-Bahn: Alexanderplatz.*

❻ Marienkirche. Opposite the fountain stands the late-13th-century Marienkirche, Berlin's

Neptune towers above the nymphs at the Neptunbrunnen.

second-oldest church after **Nikolaikirche** (p 9). Note the baroque steeple, an 18th-century addition by architect Carl Gotthard Langhans of Brandenburg Gate fame. The vaulted interior hides a sublime alabaster pulpit (1703), decorated with reliefs personifying faith, hope, and love. Near the entrance is the *Dance of Death*, a 15th-century fresco symbolizing the bubonic plague that struck Europe in the Dark Ages. ⏱ *20 min. Karl-Liebknecht-Strasse 8. ☎ 030-242-44-67. Admission free. Daily 10am–6pm. S-Bahn: Alexanderplatz.*

❼ ★ Rotes Rathaus. Just across the way is Berlin's town hall, built in the 1860s with an Italian Renaissance twist. A filigree gate, stained-glass windows, and columns guide your eye to the central 74m (242 ft.) tower. Its architectural antithesis, the **Fernsehturm** (p 49), pops up right behind. Time permitting, return at dusk when the bricks turn a deep shade of terracotta. ⏱ *15 min. Rathausstrasse 15. S-Bahn: Alexanderplatz.*

❽ ★★ Fernsehturm. Berlin's so-called *Telespargel* ("TV asparagus"), on Alexanderplatz, is impossible to ignore. If its steel sphere glinting in the sunshine doesn't grab your attention, its iconic wink after dark surely will. But the giant relic of the GDR is best appreciated with a speedy ascent to its 200m (656 ft.) viewing platform, from where the city spreads out below. ⏱ *45 min. See p 49.*

❾ ★ Alexanderplatz & the World Clock. Alfred Döblin penned a crime novel about it, the GDR government turned it into a showcase for their trademark tower blocks, and Berliners affectionately dubbed it Alex. Just don't expect a beautiful square: Prefab 1960s monoliths are a throwback to when Alexanderplatz was the epicenter of East Berlin. It does, though, have a certain urban charm with its rattling trams and eternal buzz. A popular gathering place is the revolving World Clock, crowned by a model of the solar system that tells the time in 24 time zones. ⏱ *15 min. S-Bahn: Alexanderplatz.*

The World Clock is a popular meeting place on Berlin's Alexanderplatz.

❿ ★ kids Nikolaiviertel. Leave the commotion behind and slip into a more leisurely pace in the Nikolaiviertel, a 1979 recreation of Berlin's medieval birthplace. Though it can feel twee and touristy at times, the cobbled streets are an escape from the big-city buzz. One of the few original buildings still standing is the twin-spired Nikolaikirche, Berlin's oldest church dating to 1230 (p 9, **❾**). On the banks of the River Spree, the 19th-century Kurfürstenhaus (Electoral House), a step-gabled townhouse in German neo-Renaissance style, leads through to a tranquil courtyard. The dusky pink **Knoblauchhaus** (Garlic House) nearby is Berlin's best-preserved 18th-century patrician house. Also worth a peek is the **Ephraim-Palais,** a grand rococo townhouse built by Friedrich Wilhelm Diterichs for the affluent merchant Veitel Heine Ephraim in 1765. With its slender pillars and gilded filigree balconies, locals came to call this the *schönste Ecke Berlins* (Berlin's most beautiful corner). ⏱ *1½ hr. S-Bahn: Alexanderplatz.*

Grin & Bear it

Brown bears have been Berlin's official mascot since 1280, appearing on the city's flag and coat of arms. There are many tales of how they came to represent Berlin, but one of the most plausible is that Berlin sounds like *Bär* (bear). South of the Nikolaiviertel, in the greenery of Köllnischer Park, kids will be all smiles when they come face to face with Maxi and her daughter, Schnute, in the bear pit. You can visit the bears for free anytime during daylight hours and might be lucky enough to see them feeding.

⓫ ★ Franziskaner-Klosterkirche.
A short amble east of Nikolaiviertel brings you to the redbrick remains of this eerie Franciscan monastery church (1250). The three-winged basilica became a grammar school in 1574 during the Protestant Reformation, later spawning such talent as architect Karl Friedrich Schinkel (1781–1841) and Germany's first chancellor, Otto von Bismarck (1815–98). Silence always reigns at this Gothic edifice, which was heavily bombed in World War II and is

The Franziskaner-Klosterkirche—a little-known gem close to Alexanderplatz.

today little more than a shell with a blasted roof and shattered walls. Step inside to admire the Fernsehturm through the arches, or glimpse the sculpture of Jesus removing his crown of thorns near the entrance. 🕐 *20 min. Klosterstrasse 73a.* ☎ *030-636-12-13. May–Nov Tues–Sun noon–6pm. U-Bahn: Klosterstrasse.*

⓬ Alte Stadtmauer. If you thought Berlin's only wall was the one that came down in 1989, you might be surprised to discover what remains of the medieval city walls tucked down this quiet street. It's not much to look at, but alas this is all that remains of ramparts that completely ringed Berlin in the 14th century. 🕐 *10 min. Littenstrasse. U-Bahn: Klosterstrasse.*

⓭ ★ Zur Letzten Instanz. This wayside inn of yore has served up carnivorous staples since 1621. Rest weary feet by the tiled oven that once warmed Napoleon, and tuck into schnitzel or pork knuckles. *See p 116.* €€€.

Museum **Island**

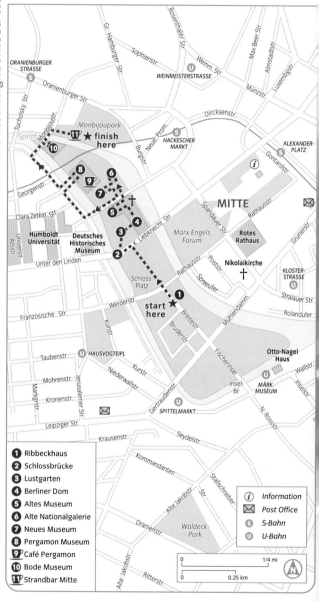

1. Ribbeckhaus
2. Schlossbrücke
3. Lustgarten
4. Berliner Dom
5. Altes Museum
6. Alte Nationalgalerie
7. Neues Museum
8. Pergamon Museum
9. Café Pergamon
10. Bode Museum
11. Strandbar Mitte

(i) Information
✉ Post Office
Ⓢ S-Bahn
Ⓤ U-Bahn

0   1/4 mi
0   0.25 km

Waving the UNESCO World Heritage flag for Berlin, Museum Island has enough architecture, art, and antique gems to satisfy anyone's cultural cravings. Be transported back to Ancient Greece at the steps of the Pergamon Altar, or trace the brushstrokes of Cézanne at the Alte Nationalgalerie. The greenery of Lustgarten and sundowners beside the Spree offer respite for museum-weary feet. START: **U-Bahn to Märkisches Museum.**

1 Ribbeckhaus. It's worth starting slightly south of Museum Island to find the gabled Ribbeckhaus, one of Berlin's best-preserved late-Renaissance edifices dating back to 1624. The ornamental facade recalls its grand past when it was home to the noble privy councilor Hans Georg von Ribbeck and his wife Katharina von Brösicke. ⏰ *15 min. Breite Strasse 35. U-Bahn: Märkisches Museum.*

2 Schlossbrücke. With its trio of arches and dreamy river views, Karl Friedrich Schinkel's early-19th-century bridge linking Unter den Linden to Schlossplatz is a walkable work of art. Cross it to glimpse mythological Greek goddesses Athena and Nike sculpted from white marble and perched on pedestals. Morning and dusk are the best time to photograph the bridge with the Berliner

Dom in the background. ⏰ *10 min. S-Bahn: Hackescher Markt.*

3 kids Lustgarten. Sweeping up to the Berliner Dom and Altes Museum, this manicured garden on the banks of the Spree is a fine spot for lounging. Framed by lime trees, with a central fountain, the Lustgarten was the pleasure garden of the Hohenzollern royals in the 16th century. ⏰ *15 min. Schlossplatz. S-Bahn: Hackescher Markt.*

4 ★ Berliner Dom. After a leisurely start, you're probably still fizzing with energy. You'll certainly need some puff to climb the 267 steps to the top of the dome of Berlin's neo-baroque cathedral, built between 1895 and 1905. High up beside the angels, the vistas reward your efforts, reaching from the Rotes Rathaus to the Reichstag and

The greenery of Lustgarten is the perfect spot to appreciate the Berliner Dom.

The opulent interior of the neo-Renaissance Berliner Dom.

beyond. The exit leads through the crypt, where ornate sarcophagi include that of King Frederick III (1415–93), the last emperor to be crowned in Rome by a pope, in 1452. 🕐 *45 min. See p 9.*

⑤ ★★ kids Altes Museum. Designed by Karl Friedrich Schinkel and built between 1823 and 1830, this museum is visually striking. Its fluted Ionic columns draw inspiration from the architecture of Ancient Athens and its central rotunda from the Pantheon in Rome. Inside, the vast repository of classical antiquities includes Greek sculptures, jewelry and silverware, and a world-renowned collection of Etruscan and Roman art. The upper floor showcases treasures from late-Hellenistic cremation urns and sarcophagi to mosaics, mummy portraits, and other treasures. For discounts on museums, see p 168. 🕐 *1 hr. Am Lustgarten.* ☎ *030-20-90-55-77. Admission 8€ adults, 4€ concessions, free for children under 18. Daily 10am–6pm, Thurs until 10pm. S-Bahn: Hackescher Markt.*

⑥ ★★★ Alte Nationalgalerie. Make a date with the 18th- to early-20th-century masters at the Old National Gallery. The backdrop is as magnificent as the works on display, with mosaic floors, frescoed ceilings, and stucco flourishes. A spin through the permanent collection on the 1st floor takes in brooding Realist works by German painter Adolph Menzel (1815–1905). Head up to the 2nd floor to admire French Impressionist paintings from the likes of Monet (1840–1926), Renoir (1841–1919), and Degas (1834–1917), alongside an outstanding collection of works by German-Jewish artist Max Liebermann (1847–1935). 🕐 *1 hr. Bodestrasse.* ☎ *030-20-90-55-77. Admission 8€ adults, 4€ concessions, free for children under 18. Tues–Sun 10am–6pm. S-Bahn: Hackescher Markt.*

⑦ ★★★ kids Neues Museum. The Neues Museum reopened in October 2009 to much acclaim with

All Aboard!

From April to October, BWTS (☎ 030-65-88-02-03) operate water taxis for a 1-hour chug along the River Spree, past the Pergamon Museum, Bode Museum, and Siegessäule. The nearest embarkation point to Museum Island is Domaquarée on Karl-Liebknecht-Brücke, opposite the Berliner Dom. Tours costs 9€ adults, 3€ for children under 12; the first is at 10:15am and the last at 5:15pm. For more details, see www.berliner-wassertaxi.de.

a makeover based on Friedrich August Stüler's original mid-19th-century, neoclassical design and centered on two magnificent courtyards adorned with classical friezes. Pride and joy is the Egyptian collection's papyruses, mummy masks, hieroglyphics, and statuary. Most entrancing of all is the enigmatic bust of Nefertiti (around 1350 B.C.), wife of Egypt's Pharaoh Akhenaten, in room 210. The museum also shelters Prehistory and Early History collections, with highlights such as the Neanderthal skull from Le Moustier and Heinrich Schliemann's collection of Trojan antiquities. Avoid the queues by purchasing a time-slot ticket online or by phone. *1 hr. Bodestrasse. 030-266-42-42-42. www.neues-museum.de. Admission 10€ adults, 5€ concessions, free for children under 18. Sun–Wed 10am–6pm, Thurs–Sat 10am–8pm. S-Bahn: Hackescher Markt.*

8 ★★★ kids Pergamon Museum. Climb the polished steps of the Pergamon Altar to gaze on graceful Ionic columns and a frieze of Greek gods battling Titans. Other must-sees include the Babylonian Ishtar Gate, embellished with unicorns and dragons, and the Market Gate of Miletus dating from A.D. 120, once the entrance to the ancient city of Miletus in Western Anatolia (today Aydın province in southwestern Turkey). Excavated in the 19th century, the gate was transported piece by piece to the Pergamon, where it has been meticulously reconstructed. *1 hr. See p 8.*

9 Café Pergamon. Grab a table on the sunny terrace of this museum cafe for a quick coffee or snack, such as baked potatoes and goat's cheese *Knödel* (dumplings). 030-20-90-63-61. €.

10 Bode Museum. This is worth a visit if only to gawp at the palatial interior of marble pilasters and wrought-iron banisters. Decorative arts are in for a treat, with Renaissance altarpieces, Prussian ivory and cameos, Byzantine art, and medieval sculptures aplenty. Look out for the tiny 16th-century figurine depicting the goddess Venus. *1 hr. Am Kupfergraben 1. 030-20-90-55-77. Admission 8€ adults, 4€ concessions, free for children under 18. Daily 10am–6pm, Thurs until 10pm. U-Bahn: Friedrichstrasse.*

11 ★ Strandbar Mitte. Facing the Bode Museum, this beach on the Costa del Spree is perfect for summertime chilling. Recline in a deckchair under the palms, caipirnha in hand, as DJs spin mellow grooves. *Monbijoustrasse 3. 030-28-38-55-88. S-Bahn: Oranienburger Strasse. €€.*

The domed Bode Museum overlooks the Spree River.

Kreuzberg

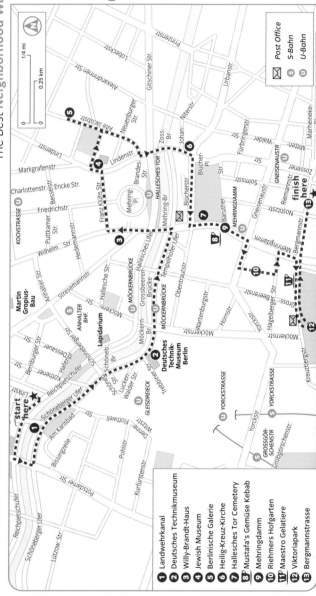

1 Landwehrkanal
2 Deutsches Technikmuseum
3 Willy-Brandt-Haus
4 Jewish Museum
5 Berlinische Galerie
6 Heilig-Kreuz-Kirche
7 Hallesches Tor Cemetery
8 Mustafa's Gemüse Kebab
9 Mehringdamm
10 Riehmers Hofgarten
11 Maestro Gelatiere
12 Viktoriapark
13 Bergmannstrasse

Post Office
S-Bahn
U-Bahn

start here

finish here

Once the economic runt of the litter in former West Berlin, Kreuzberg is now one of the city's most vibrant neighborhoods, known for its upbeat nightlife, bohemian cafes, and shabby-chic boutiques attracting an alternative, arty crowd. This walk takes you from the quiet Landwehrkanal to party-loving Bergmannstrasse.

START: **U-Bahn to Mendelssohn-Bartholdy-Park.**

1 **kids** **Landwehrkanal.** Enjoy some fresh air with a brisk walk along the tree-fringed Landwehrkanal. Cutting a 12km (7 miles) path through Berlin, the canal is a green retreat in the heart of the city. Don't expect solitude, though; the shady paths are popular with locals from dog walkers to rollerbladers, cyclists, and even the odd sunbather in warmer months. ⏱ *20 min. U-Bahn: Mendelssohn-Bartholdy-Park.*

2 ★★ **kids** **Deutsches Technikmuseum.** A silver DC-3 plane guides the way to this cavernous technology museum. Technically minded whiz-kids are in their element faced with everything from nostalgic steam trains to marvelous flying contraptions. Keep an eye out for the 19th-century Dutch windmill in the garden. ⏱ *1 hr. See p 28.*

3 **Willy-Brandt-Haus.** This striking glass-and-limestone building is a fitting tribute to Willy Brandt, the former chancellor of West Germany (1969–74) and Nobel Peace Prize winner. In the entrance stands a

Snow surrounding the Jewish Museum.

bronze of the politician himself, who endeavored to improve relations with the East through his *Ostpolitik* policy. Now the headquarters of the Social Democratic Party, the building hosts temporary exhibitions and cultural events. ⏱ *30 min. Wilhelmstrasse 140.* ☎ *030-25-99-37-00. Tues–Sun 10am–6pm, Admission free. U-Bahn: Hallesches Tor.*

Carnival of Cultures

Every year on the last weekend in May, Kreuzberg celebrates its diversity with a Carnival of Cultures, when acrobats, magicians, and flamboyant dancers take to the streets. The free street festival attracts a huge number of partygoers. One minute it's soca rhythms, the next you're swaying to merengue or roaming an oriental bazaar. Expect parades, concerts, and club nights a-plenty. For the latest lineup, see **www.karneval-berlin.de** or call ☎ 030-609-77-00.

Berlinische Galerie.

4 ★★★ **Jewish Museum.** Step inside Daniel Libeskind's shimmering museum for an emotional trip through the past and present of Jewish Germany; from the chilling corridors of the Axis of Holocaust to the permanent exhibition upstairs celebrating famous sons such as the Romantic composer and conductor Felix Mendelssohn-Bartholdy (1809–47). ⏱ *1 hr. See p 16.*

5 ★★ **Berlinische Galerie.** This modernist gallery, housed in a former glass warehouse, is particularly strong on styles such as the Berlin Secession, New Objectivity, and Expressionism. Look out for works by Otto Dix, George Grosz, and Max Liebermann. ⏱ *1 hr. See p 38.*

6 **Heilig-Kreuz-Kirche.** Amble south onto Zossener Strasse and you'll notice the wistful spires, 19m-high (62 ft.) cupola, and rosy hue of this little-known evangelical church. Light floods the rose window of this neo-Gothic beauty built between 1884 and 1888 by German architect Johannes Otzen. Keep an eye out for Ismond Rosen's 1996

triptych sculpture *Christus im Holocaust* (Christ in the Holocaust). ⏱ *20 min. Zossener Strasse 65. Mon 9am–3pm, Tues–Fri 9am–7pm, Sat 3–6pm, Sun 9am–6pm. U-Bahn: Hallesches Tor.*

7 **Hallesches Tor Cemetery.** Across the street, an 18th-century cemetery hides a shrine for classical music pilgrims. As you enter, veer left to find the white cross marking the grave of the prominent Romantic composer and conductor Felix Mendelssohn-Bartholdy (1809–47), who had composed 12 string symphonies by the age of 14. His famous works include the *String Octet* (1825) and overture to Shakespeare's *A Midsummer Night's Dream* (1826). The composer is buried close to his sister, Fanny Hensel Mendelssohn, also a gifted composer and pianist. Overgrown with ivy and shaded by trees, the rest of the silent graveyard is scattered with graceful Art Nouveau funerary sculptures. ⏱ *20 min. Mehringdamm 21. No phone. Summer 8am–8pm; winter 8am–4pm. U-Bahn: Mehringdamm.*

8 Mustafa's Gemüse Kebab. Mustafa's vegetarian kebab stand right in front of the U-Bahn station is a Kreuzberg favorite for its fresh ingredients and pocket-pleasing prices. *Mehringdamm U-Bahn.* €.

9 Mehringdamm. Kreuzberg's main drag is a great place to get a feel for this offbeat, ethnic neighborhood. It's dotted with good-value snack bars where you can stop for a *Currywurst*, falafel, or kebab. On and around Mehringdamm, one-off specialty shops, boho cafes, and bars invite exploration. ⏱ *20 min. U-Bahn: Mehringdamm.*

10 ★★ Riehmers Hofgarten. Leave the hubbub of Mehringdamm behind by passing through a wrought-iron gate and taking a stroll through this sublime Art Nouveau courtyard, lined with elegant 19th-century townhouses. ⏱ *15 min. See p 16.*

11 kids Maestro Gelatiere. Pop into this Italian ice cream parlor for unusual-flavor *gelato* such as chestnut or ginger, before heading across to Viktoriapark opposite. *Kreuzbergstrasse 13.* ☎ *030-78-89-71-75.* €.

The wrought iron detail of the gates to Riehmers Hofgarten in Kreuzberg.

12 ★ kids Viktoriapark. This leafy park is where Kreuzbergers from all walks of life come when the sun's out. Enjoy a picnic by the waterfall, or climb up to the 66m (217 ft.) viewing point for a panorama of Berlin. ⏱ *30 min. See p 48.*

13 ★ Bergmannstrasse. Time and energy permitting, you can round off your day on Kreuzberg's lively bar mile. One of my favorites is underground, über-cool **Bar Nou** (p 128), where the expert mixologists serve a refreshing Shaolin Iced Tea. *U-Bahn: Mehringdamm.*

Spa Time

Need to give your feet a rest? For an indulgent Turkish bath, scrub or olive oil massage, head over to Sultan Hamam (Bülowstrasse 57; ☎ 030-21-75-33-75; www.sultan-hamam.de). Most days are for women only, except on Sundays when it's mixed and Mondays when it's men only. Alternatively, **Liquidrom** (Möckernstrasse 10; ☎ 030-258-00-78-20; www.liquidrom-berlin.de) is a day spa with minimalist decor, subtle lighting, and underwater classical music lulling you into relaxation. You can drift away in the domed saltwater pool, with a Himalayan salt sauna or a soothing Balinese massage.

Kurfürstendamm & Around

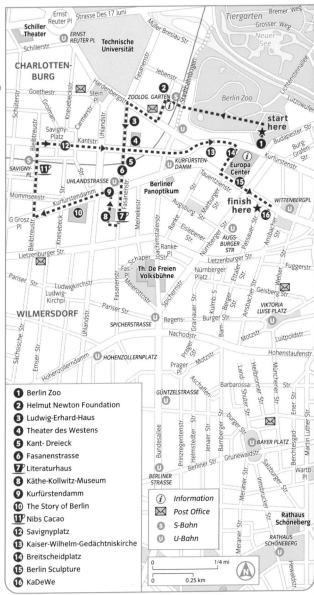

1. Berlin Zoo
2. Helmut Newton Foundation
3. Ludwig-Erhard-Haus
4. Theater des Westens
5. Kant- Dreieck
6. Fasanenstrasse
7. Literaturhaus
8. Käthe-Kollwitz-Museum
9. Kurfürstendamm
10. The Story of Berlin
11. Nibs Cacao
12. Savignyplatz
13. Kaiser-Wilhelm-Gedächtniskirche
14. Breitscheidplatz
15. Berlin Sculpture
16. KaDeWe

i   Information
✉   Post Office
Ⓢ   S-Bahn
Ⓤ   U-Bahn

0   1/4 mi
0   0.25 km

This classic shop and stroll through well-heeled Charlottenburg begins at the zoo, before moving to Kantstrasse for a feast of classic and contemporary architecture. Take in Art Nouveau villas and Käthe Kollwitz's art on Fasanenstrasse, and then get your boutique and chocolate fix on Savignyplatz before hitting the shops on Kurfürstendamm itself. START: U-Bahn to Zoologischer Garten.

1 ★ kids **Berlin Zoo.** If your kids are tired of grown-up stuff, take them to visit Berlin's zoo. Two stone elephants guard the pagoda-style gate, behind which the gardens play host to spacious animal enclosures. Take your little ones to see the penguins, sea lions, zebras, and bubble-blowing hippos, as well as rarities like the flightless kiwi bird, indigenous to New Zealand. ⏱ 1½ hr. See p 26. U-Bahn: Zoologischer Garten.

2 ★ **Helmut Newton Foundation.** Tucked behind Zoologischer Garten S-Bahn station, this museum zooms in on prolific fashion photographer Helmut Newton (1920–2004), whose images graced the pages of fashion magazines like Vanity Fair and Vogue. Born in Berlin to a German-Jewish father, Newton was

Tots love to clamber over the stone elephant guarding the gates to Berlin Zoo.

forced to flee the city in 1938. Alongside some of his famous nudes, the display shows items from his private life—from his reconstructed Monte Carlo office to calendars, posters, and letters. ⏱ 1 hr. Jebensstrasse 2. ☎ 030-31-86-48-56. www.helmutnewton.com. Admission 6€ adults, 3€ concessions. Tues–Sun 10am–6pm; to 10pm Thurs. S-Bahn: Zoologischer Garten.

3 **Ludwig-Erhard-Haus.** Across the way, you can't miss British architect Sir Nicholas Grimshaw's modernist edifice, designed in 1994 to house the Chamber of Commerce and Berlin Stock Exchange. The exterior gives the appearance of a giant armadillo—this organic form supposedly symbolizes the living "organism" of the stock market. ⏱ 10 min. Fasanenstrasse 83–84. S-Bahn: Zoologischer Garten.

4 **Theater des Westens.** Soaring pillars, wreath-bearing cherubs, and lavish stucco epitomize turn-of-the-century grandeur at this Kantstrasse theater. Luminaries such as actress Marlene Dietrich and French-American singer Josephine Baker have graced the stage over the years. Pause to admire the facade: A mélange of Renaissance, Art Nouveau, and Empire styles, built by Bernhard Sehring in 1895. ⏱ 10 min. See p 138.

5 **Kant-Dreieck.** Walking west along Kantstrasse, Josef Paul Kleihues' 36m (118 ft.) gneiss-and-steel tower, graced by a sail-like Dreieck (triangle), forces you to look up.

The steel arches of Ludwig-Erhard-Haus resemble the bony armour of an armadillo.

⏱ *10 min. Kantstrasse 155. S-Bahn: Zoologischer Garten.*

⑥ ★★ **Fasanenstrasse.** Stretching from Charlottenburger Tor to Hohenzollerndamm, this elegant street takes its name from the 18th-century *Fasanerie* (royal pheasant house) of King Friedrich II. Lined with galleries, and smart boutiques, Fasanenstrasse is one of Charlottenburg's smartest avenues. It's also a hive of creativity, drawing local artists and authors. Amble south to Fasanenplatz, a leafy square flanked by typical Art Nouveau townhouses. Slightly farther along is the one-time residence of author Heinrich Mann (no. 61), brother of Nobel Laureate Thomas, who in 1905 penned *Professor Unrat*. His book was the inspiration for *The Blue Angel*, the film that brought Marlene Dietrich to world renown. ⏱ *1 hr. Fasanenstrasse. U-Bahn: Uhlandstrasse.*

⑦ **Literaturhaus.** Local authors gather for coffee and intelligent conversation at this cafe/bookshop, which was formally a military hospital,

soup kitchen, and brothel. Come for fireside readings or the leafy garden in warmer weather. *Fasanenstrasse 23.* ☎ *030-882-54-14.* €.

⑧ ★ **Käthe-Kollwitz-Museum.** Contemplate the emotive, brooding works of German painter and sculptor Käthe Kollwitz (1867–1945) in this gem of a museum. Set in a gorgeous 19th-century villa, the collection comprises graphics, lithographs, woodcuts, and sculptures that reveal recurring dark themes. *Brot!* (1924) and *The Call of Death* (1934–35) are particularly touching. ⏱ *45 min. Fasanenstrasse 24.* ☎ *030-882-52-10. www.kaethe-kollwitz.de. Admission 6€ adults, 3€ concessions. Daily 11am–6pm. U-Bahn: Uhlandstrasse.*

⑨ ★★ **kids** **Kurfürstendamm.** Simply Ku'damm to locals, this royal bridle path turned shopping mile is one of Berlin's most elegant boulevards. Go west for swish designer boutiques such as **Budapester Schuhe** (p 94), Gucci, Cartier, and Valentino. The eastern stretch, where Ku'damm meets Tauentzienstrasse, is given over to department stores and high-street brands such as Benetton, **Camper** (p 94), and Diesel. ⏱ *45 min. Kurfürstendamm. U-Bahn: Uhlandstrasse.*

⑩ ★ **kids** **The Story of Berlin.** This interactive museum chronicles Berlin's history using photos, film, costumes, and audio effects. You start with the founding of the city in the 13th century and move swiftly to Prussia, the Industrial Revolution, the Third Reich, and the Berlin Wall. The highlight is an original nuclear air-raid shelter. It's a fun, touchy-feely way of exploring Berlin's past that kids will love. ⏱ *45 min. Kurfürstendamm 207–208.* ☎ *030-88-72-01-00. www.story-of-berlin.de.*

Admission 10€ adults, 8€ concessions, 5€ children under 13. Daily 10am–8pm. U-Bahn: Uhlandstrasse.

11 ★ kids **Nibs Cacao.** The hot chocolate here is dark, smooth, and totally divine. Choose from varieties including Spanish-style with *churros* to American-style with marshmallows. *Bleibtreustrasse 46.* ☎ 030-34-72-63-00. €.

12 **Savignyplatz.** Wandering east you hit this square linking Kantstrasse and Ku'damm, framed by bars and restaurants. The southern side shelters the Else-Ury-Bogen, redbrick railway arches that harbor one-off fashion boutiques, bookstores, and designer shops. Head south along Bleibtreustrasse to pick up everything from oriental art and antiques to flamboyant costume jewelry and sassy designer wear. ⏱ *30 min. S-Bahn: Savignyplatz.*

13 ★★ **Kaiser-Wilhelm-Gedächtniskirche.** The ruins of the original 19th-century structure (damaged badly in World War II) adjoins a modern octagonal church, designed by German architect Egon Eiermann in 1961. Step inside to view a monumental golden statue of the resurrected Christ suspended above the altar, with his arms outstretched in the form of a cross. The church was closed for renovation at the time of writing but was expected to reopen in mid-2012. ⏱ *45 min. Breitscheidplatz.* ☎ *030-78-89-11-01. Admission free. Daily 9am–7pm. U-Bahn: Kurfürstendamm.*

14 ★ kids **Breitscheidplatz.** Sandwiched between Ku'damm and Tauentzienstrasse, this square is dwarfed by the multi-story Europa Center shopping mall (p 89)— but even more striking is the **Weltkugelbrunnen fountain** that

Delicious chocolate lures the sweet-toothed into Nibs Cacao.

Berliners nickname *Wasserklops* (water dumpling), a red granite globe designed by Joachim Schmettau in 1983. ⏱ *15 min. U-Bahn: Kurfürstendamm*

15 **Berlin Sculpture.** Opposite the church is Brigitte and Martin Matschinsky-Denninghoff's wacky open-air artwork. The sculpture's shiny steel tendrils twist up to intertwine above a patch of greenery on Tauentzienstrasse. Erected to mark Berlin's 750th anniversary in 1987, the broken chain is a powerful symbol of a city divided yet inextricably linked. ⏱ *15 min. Tauentzienstrasse. U-Bahn: Kurfürstendamm.*

16 ★★ **KaDeWe.** A few paces farther down Tauentzienstrasse is the grandest and largest of Berlin's department stores, KaDeWe, where well-heeled locals have been shopping since 1907. Seven floors cover everything from interior design to designer fashion. The 6th-floor food hall offers a gourmet wonderland of truffles, pates, preserves, oysters, wine, and irresistible tortes. *See p 89.*

Unter den Linden & Around

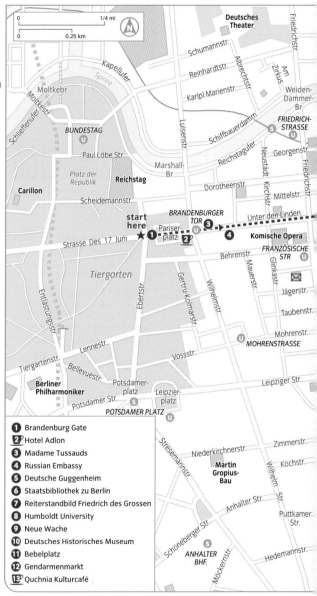

1 Brandenburg Gate
2 Hotel Adlon
3 Madame Tussauds
4 Russian Embassy
5 Deutsche Guggenheim
6 Staatsbibliothek zu Berlin
7 Reiterstandbild Friedrich des Grossen
8 Humboldt University
9 Neue Wache
10 Deutsches Historisches Museum
11 Bebelplatz
12 Gendarmenmarkt
13 Quchnia Kulturcafé

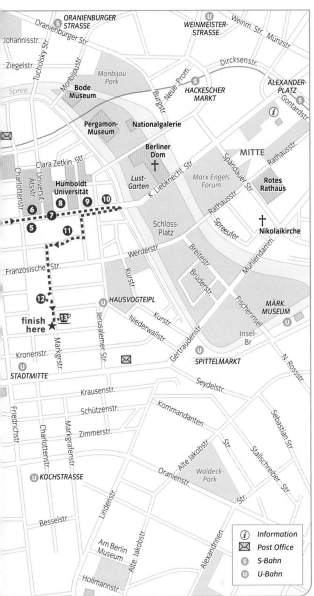

Map labels:

ORANIENBURGER STRASSE
Oranienburger Str.
Johannisstr.
Ziegelstr.
Tucholsky Str.
Monbijoustr.
Monbijou Park
Bode Museum
Spree
Pergamon-Museum
Nationalgalerie
Clara Zetkin Str.
Charlottenstr.
Universit
Atsstr.
Humboldt Universität
Berliner Dom
Lust-Garten
Schloss-Platz
Werderstr.
Französische Str.
finish here
Kronenstr.
Markgrstr.
STADTMITTE
Krausenstr.
Schützenstr.
Zimmerstr.
Friedrichstr.
Charlottenstr.
Markgrafenstr.
KOCHSTRASSE
Besselstr.
Lindenstr.
Am Berlin Museum
Alte Jakobstr.
Hollmannstr.

WEINMEISTER-STRASSE
Weinm. Str. Münzstr.
Dircksenstr.
Neue Prom.
Burgstr.
HACKESCHER MARKT
ALEXANDER-PLATZ
Gontardstr.
MITTE
K. Liebknecht Str.
Spandauer Str.
Marx Engels Forum
Rathausstr.
Rotes Rathaus
Rathausstr.
Spreeufer
Breitestr.
Brüderstr.
Nikolaikirche
Mühlendamm
Fischerinsel
MÄRK. MUSEUM
Insel-Br
Kurstr.
HAUSVOGTEIPL
Niederwallstr.
Jerusalemer Str.
Gertraudenstr.
SPITTELMARKT
N. Rossstr.
Seydelstr.
Kommandanten
Alte Jakobstr. Str.
Oranienstr.
Waldeck-Park
Sebastian Str
Stallschreiber- Str.
Str.
Alexandrinen

Legend:

(i) Information
✉ Post Office
Ⓢ S-Bahn
Ⓤ U-Bahn

Stretching from the Brandenburg Gate to Museum Island, lime-tree-lined Unter den Linden is Berlin's classic strolling boulevard. Low on effort, high on sights, this classic walk takes in historic monuments, museums, and galleries en route to one of the city's most beautiful squares, Gendarmenmarkt. **START: U-Bahn to Brandenburger Tor.**

Gaze up at the Doric columns of the Brandenburg Gate, bathed gold at dusk.

① ★★★ **Brandenburg Gate.** This triumphal gateway is most impressive first thing in the morning or at dusk. Its imposing Doric columns and its crowning glory, quadriga, are ideally photographed from Pariser Platz. *See p 7. U-Bahn: Brandenburger Tor.*

② **Hotel Adlon.** Berlin's poshest terrace cafe (p 147), affords peerless views of the Brandenburg Gate. The hotel has rolled out the red carpet for the likes of Charlie Chaplin, Michael Jackson, and Greta Garbo over the years. *Unter den Linden 77.* ☎ *030-226-10.* €€€.

③ kids ★★ **Madame Tussauds.** Famous Germans from Einstein and film diva Marlene Dietrich to Pope Benedict appear in all their realistic glory at this new Madame Tussauds. You're free to take photographs of the waxworks, with the exception of Adolf Hitler who is, in an ironic twist of fate, confined to a box. Save time by buying tickets in advance online. ⏱ *1½ hr. Unter den Linden 74. www. madametussauds.com/berlin. Admission 19.90€ adults, 14.90€ children under 14. U-Bahn: Brandenburger Tor.*

④ **Russian Embassy.** On the opposite side of the street you'll see the tower and sharp angles of the Russian Embassy—built in the 1950s, in typical Stalinist wedding-cake style. ⏱ *10 min. Unter den Linden 63–65. S-Bahn: Unter den Linden.*

⑤ ★ **Deutsche Guggenheim.** On the corner of Friedrichstrasse, the Guggenheim stages three or four major exhibitions of modern or contemporary art each year (there's no permanent collection). There are free guided tours in German at 6pm daily. ⏱ *45 min. Unter den Linden 13–15.* ☎ *030-202-09-30. www. deutsche-guggenheim-berlin.de. Admission 4€ adults, 3€ concessions, free for children under 12. Daily 10am–8pm. S-Bahn: Unter den Linden.*

⑥ Staatsbibliothek zu Berlin. Next up on the left is a secret too good to keep: The inner courtyard of Berlin's neo-baroque State Library, which provides cool, quiet respite from Unter den Linden's crowds. Join the locals to recline on the benches with a book. The cavernous library (closed to the public) houses the world's largest Mozart collection and the handwritten scores of Beethoven's Symphonies Nos. 5 and 9. ⏱ *20 min. Unter den Linden 8. U-Bahn: Friedrichstrasse.*

⑦ Reiterstandbild Friedrich des Grossen. German sculptor Christian Daniel Rauch's bombastic statue of Friedrich the Great, or "old Fritz" as Berliners call him, was unveiled in 1851 to mark the Prussian king's ascension to the throne. Mounted on a fine horse and looking rather dashing, Fritz perches on a podium, embossed with reliefs depicting scenes from his life. He was a powerful ruler, famed for increasing Prussia's prestige and promoting religious tolerance. *Unter den Linden. U-Bahn: Friedrichstrasse.*

⑧ ★ Humboldt University. Berlin's renowned seat of learning has been in the global spotlight by winning 29 Nobel prizes and accommodating some of Germany's biggest brains, among them physicist Albert Einstein, Otto von Bismarck (the "Iron Chancellor"), poet Heinrich Heine, and even Marx and Engels

(p 53, ⑤). Most days there's a second-hand book market (times vary) in the courtyard. *Unter den Linden 6. U-Bahn: Friedrichstrasse.*

⑨ ★★ Neue Wache. Light streams through a skylight to illuminate Käthe Kollwitz's *Mutter mit totem Sohn*, a sculpture of a grieving mother holding her dead son. Dating back to 1816, the austere Neue Wache (New Guardhouse) is today dedicated to the victims of war and tyranny, and contains the remains of an unknown soldier and a concentration camp prisoner, surrounded by earth from World War II battlefields and camps. *Unter den Linden 4. U-Bahn: Friedrichstrasse.*

⑩ ★★★ Deutsches Historisches Museum. The baroque Zeughaus (old arsenal) of Brandenburg Elector Frederick III that dominates the corner of Unter den Linden shelters the DHM (German History Museum). The collection

Berlin's classic strolling boulevard, Unter den Linden.

The Deutsches Historisches Museum provides a fascinating insight into German history.

stretches deep into the vault of history, including displays of Celtic jewelry, Roman codices, Habsburg portraits, and World War II propaganda posters. Fascinating exhibits include the 15th-century *Behan Globus*, one of the first globes to depict a round earth. On the 2nd floor, seek out Napoleon's bicorn hat and sword, which Prussian soldiers discovered after he ran from the Battle of Waterloo in 1815. A stunning architectural addition is the adjacent glass spiral construction, designed by the award-winning Chinese-American architect I.M. Pei to host temporary exhibitions. 🕐 *1½ hr. Unter den Linden 2.* ☎ *030-20-30-44-44. www.dhm.de. Admission 6€ adults, free for children under 18. Daily 10am–6pm. U-Bahn: Französische Strasse.*

⓫ ★★ Bebelplatz. It was right here on the cobbles of Bebelplatz that the Nazi book burning took place on May 10, 1933, when 20,000 works from the likes of Austrian psychiatrist Sigmund Freud and German playwright Bertolt Brecht went up in flames. Under the orders of Nazi Propaganda Minister, Joseph Goebbels, right-wing students, and SA (Storm Section) officers publicly burned literary works considered Jewish, communist, or degenerate in a bid to "purify" Germany. A small plaque at the center of the square commemorates the prophetic words of Romantic poet Heinrich Heine: *Dort, wo man Bücher verbrennt, verbrennt man am Ende auch Menschen* (Where you burn books today, you burn people tomorrow). The exact spot is marked by Micha Ullmann's extraordinary underground empty bookshelves monument (p 32). Tucked behind the neoclassical Staatsoper Unter den Linden (the opera house; p 136) is another Prussian creation: The domed Hedwigskathedrale, an 18th-century cathedral inspired by the Pantheon in Rome. *Unter den Linden. U-Bahn: Französische Strasse.*

⓬ ★ Gendarmenmarkt. The best time to explore this charming square is in the evening, when street lanterns cast a glow across the cobbles. The twin baroque beauties of the Deutscher Dom and Französischer Dom flank opposite sides of the square, with Karl Friedrich Schinkel's peristyle **Konzerthaus** (p 136) and a noble statue of poet and philosopher Friedrich Schiller (1759–1805) squeezed between them. As night falls, the bistros and bars fill up with concert-goers. *U-Bahn: Französische Strasse.*

⓭ Quchnia Kulturcafé. This cafe overlooking the Deutscher Dom serves coffee with Kultur (culture) at its regular events including poetry readings and film screenings. Comfortable leather sofas and an open fire create a sleek setting for finger-food and cocktails. *Markgrafenstrasse 35.* ☎ *030-20-60-92-86. €–€€.* ●

Shopping Best Bets

Best for **Vintage Fashion**
★ Waahnsinn, *Rosenthaler Strasse 17 (p 90)*

Best **Flea Market Finds**
★ Flea Market, *Strasse des 17 Juni (p 93)*

Best for **CD Bargains**
Space Hall, *Zossener Strasse 33 (p 94)*

Best for **Diva Bling**
★★ Gallery Schrill, *Bleibtreustrasse 48 (p 93)*

Best for **Designer Dogwear**
★ Koko von Knebel, *Uhlandstrasse 181 (p 92)*

Best for **Fair-Trade Toys**
★★ Barefoot Berlin, *Kreuzbergstrasse 75 (p 94)*

Best **Urban Streetwear**
★ EASTBERLIN, *Alte Schönhauser Strasse 33–34 (p 89)*

Kids love the bright, fair-trade toys at Barefoot Berlin. Previous page: Sony Center.

Best for **Unique Truffles**
★★ Confiserie Mélanie, *Goethestrasse 4 (p 91)*

Best **One-Stop Shop**
★★★ KaDeWe, *Tauentzienstrasse 21–24 (p 89)*

Best for **Multifunctional Bags**
★★★ Tausche, *Raumerstrasse 8 (p 90)*

Best **Heaven Scents**
★★★ Parfum nach Gewicht, *Kantstrasse 106 (p 88)*

Best for **Pottery Painting**
Keramik Selber Bemahlen, *Mehringdamm 73 (p 92)*

Best **Homegrown Fashion**
★ Thatchers, *Hackesche Höfe (p 90)*

Best for **Marzipan**
★★★ Königsberger Marzipan, *Pestalozzistrasse 54a (p 91)*

Best for **Homemade Mustard**
★★ Senf Salon, *Hagelberger Strasse 46 (p 91)*

Best for **Unusual Absinthes**
★★ Absinth Depot, *Weinmeisterstrasse 4 (p 90)*

Best for **Kitsch Gifts**
★ Kwik Shop, *Kastanienallee 44 (p 92)*

Best for **Christmas Decorations**
★ Erzgebirgshaus, *Friedrichstrasse 194–199 (p 92)*

Best for **Designer Homewares**
★ House of Villeroy & Boch, *Kurfürstendamm 33 (p 88)*

Best **Traditional Sweets**
★★ Bonbonmacherei, *Oranienburger Strasse 32 (p 90)*

Charlottenburg **Shopping**

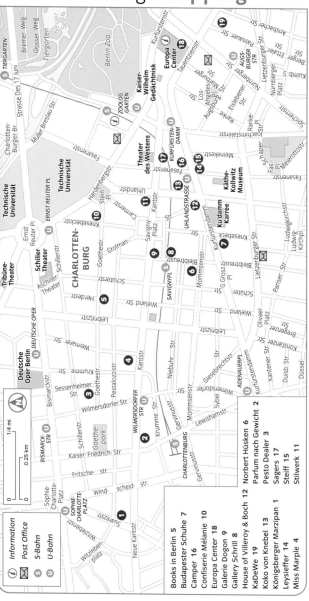

Books in Berlin 5
Budapester Schuhe 7
Camper 16
Confiserie Mélanie 10
Europa Center 18
Galerie Dogon 9
Gallery Schrill 8
House of Villeroy & Boch 12
KaDeWe 19
Koko von Knebel 13
Königsberger Marzipan 1
Leysieffer 14
Miss Marple 4
Norbert Hüsken 6
Parfum nach Gewicht 2
Pesto Dealer 3
Sagers 17
Steiff 15
Stilwerk 11

Information
Post Office
S-Bahn
U-Bahn

0   1/4 mi
0   0.25 km

Kreuzberg, Mitte, Friedrichshain & Prenzlauer Berg Shopping

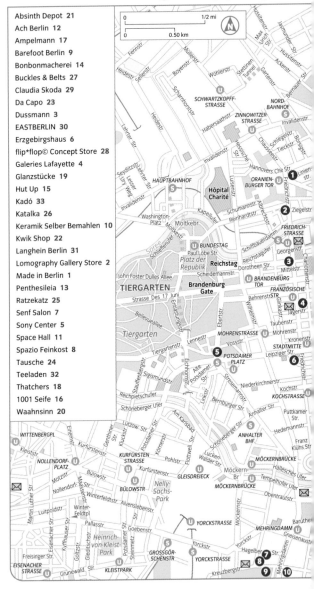

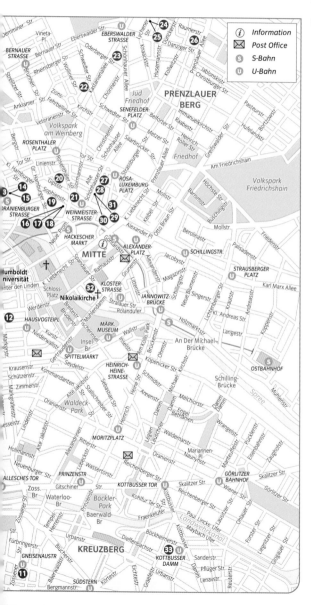

Shopping A to Z

Antiques, Art & Design
Galerie Dogon CHARLOTTEN-BURG   Berlin's top spot for intriguing African and Asian art and antiques. The collection comprises hand-carved masks, bronze amulets, jewelry, ceramics, and voodoo figurines ranging from exquisite to eerie. *Bleibtreustrasse 50.* ☎ *030-312-85-64. AE, DC, MC, V. S-Bahn: Savignyplatz. Map p 85.*

Norbert Hüsken CHARLOTTEN-BURG   This elegant store is crammed with antiques and *objets d'art* from Biedermeier to Art Deco furnishings, tableware, crystal, paintings, and porcelain. There's an emphasis on French and 19th-century antiques. *Mommsenstrasse 5.* ☎ *030-88-62-84-84. MC, V. S-Bahn: Savignyplatz. Map p 85.*

Books
kids Books in Berlin CHARLOT-TENBURG   Nip into this small, friendly bookstore to browse a high-quality selection of new, second-hand, and kids' books in English. Visit the website for details of upcoming events and author readings. *Goethestrasse 69.* ☎ *030-313-12-33. V. S-Bahn: Savignyplatz. Map p 85.*

★ Miss Marple CHARLOTTEN-BURG   Strictly for whodunnit fans, this nail-biting bookstore is filled with crime fiction classics and modern thrillers (including English-language editions) to keep you on the edge of your seat on the flight home. *Weimarer Strasse 17.* ☎ *030-36-41-27-24. No credit cards. U-Bahn: Wilmersdorfer Strasse. Map p 85.*

Ceramics & Homewares
★ House of Villeroy & Boch CHARLOTTENBURG   This temple to home design has been associated with top-quality ceramics and tableware since 1748. Designs range from classic and floral to contemporary and understated. *Kurfürstendamm 33.* ☎ *030-88-68-29-70. AE, DC, MC, V. U-Bahn: Kurfürstendamm. Map p 85.*

Cosmetics & Fragrances
★★★ Parfum nach Gewicht CHARLOTTENBURG   Follow your nose for pure, simple fragrances from patchouli to Provence lavender. All scents are weighed on brass scales and bottled in flacons (from 10g/0.3 oz.). *Kantstrasse 106.* ☎ *030-324-35-82. MC, V. U-Bahn: Wilmersdorfer Strasse. Map p 85.*

1001 Seife MITTE   An Aladdin's cave of soaps and suds, this sweet-smelling store sells plant-oil, organic, and cold-pressed soaps. The range includes mare's milk bars for soft skin and pumpkin-seed soap for a glowing complexion. *Hackesche Höfe.* ☎ *030-28-09-53-54. MC, V. S-Bahn: Hackescher Markt. Map p 86.*

Nostalgic fragrances at Parfum nach Gewicht.

Department Stores & Malls

Europa Center CHARLOTTEN-BURG   This indoor, central city mall shelters high-street stores such as Bonita and Esprit, plus snack bars, a bakery, and a hair salon. Don't miss the city view from the 20th floor. *Tauentzienstrasse 9–12.* ☎ *030-26-49-79-40. www.europa-center-berlin. de. AE, DC, MC, V. S-Bahn: Zoolo-gischer Garten. Map p 85.*

★ Galeries Lafayette

MITTE   Behind the curvy glass walls of this much-loved Parisian depart-ment store you find high-end fash-ion, fragrances, and a food hall where you can pause for oysters and champagne. *Friedrichstrasse 76.* ☎ *030-20-94-80. www.lafayette-berlin.de. AE, DC, MC, V. U-Bahn: Französische Strasse. Map p 86.*

★★★ KaDeWe CHARLOTTENBURG

High-end fashions, Meissen porcelain, and MAC cosmetics can all be found under one very elegant roof. The out-standing 6th-floor food court has an oyster bar and a cafe. *Tauentzien-strasse 21–24.* ☎ *030-21-21-0. www. kadewe.com. AE, DC, MC, V. U-Bahn: Wittenbergplatz. Map p 85.*

★ Sony Center MITTE   A soaring glass roof and dancing fountains cre-ate an ultramodern backdrop for var-ied shopping. Check out high-tech gadgets in the Sony Style Store before taking the escalator down to Pasarelle for a superjuice. *Potsdamer Strasse 4. www.sonycenter.de. AE, DC, MC, V. S-Bahn: Potsdamer Platz. Map p 86.*

★ Stilwerk CHARLOTTENBURG This glass-fronted design temple spread over four floors houses brands like Bang & Olufsen, Mösch, and Niessing. Whether you're look-ing for understated jewelry or ultra-sleek home furnishings, this is the place. *Kantstrasse 17.* ☎ *030-31-51-50. AE, MC, V. www.stilwerk.de. S-Bahn: Savignyplatz. Map p 85.*

Find high-street styles at the Europa Cen-ter mall.

Fashion

★ Claudia Skoda MITTE   You'll find the latest collection of home-grown designer Claudia Skoda at this chic boutique. From chunky sweaters to snug-fitting dresses, her colorful knitwear is elegant, femi-nine, and modern. *Alte Schönhauser Strasse 35.* ☎ *030-280-72-11. www. claudiaskoda.com. AE, MC, V. U-Bahn: Weinmeisterstrasse. Map p 86.*

★ EASTBERLIN MITTE   The kings of urban cool at this store kit you out with streetwear basics for men and women, from hand-printed hoodies to T-shirts and bags. Expect durable, eye-catching designs with bold prints and colors. *Alte Schön-hauser Strasse 33–34.* ☎ *030-24-72-39-88. AE, MC, V. U-Bahn: Weinmeisterstrasse. Map p 86.*

kids Hut Up MITTE   Presenting wildly colorful creations, Hut Up's dis-tinctive hats, bags, sweaters, dresses, and baby booties are made from raw wool using felting and blocking tech-niques. *Heckmannhöfe.* ☎ *030-28-38-61-05. AE, DC, MC, V. S-Bahn: Oranienburger Strasse. Map p 86.*

★ **Langhein Berlin** MITTE Design-conscious divas trawl this closet for floaty styles in light fabrics, from sky-blue chiffon dresses to tutu-style skirts. These fairytale fashions have even graced the Milan catwalk. *Rosa-Luxemburg-Strasse 25.* ☎ *030-442-76-97. MC, V. U-Bahn: Rosa-Luxemburg-Platz. Map p 86.*

Made in Berlin MITTE Silk scarves, secondhand clothes, shoes, and oversized 1960s shades line the shelves and walls at this hip vintage clothing store. Come during Wednesday's happy hour from 10am to 3pm for a 20% discount. *Friedrichstrasse 114a.* ☎ *030-24-04-89-00. MC, V. U-Bahn: Friedrichstrasse. Map p 86.*

★★ **Penthesileia** MITTE Anke Runge's sleek gallery-cum-workshop displays a daring collection of handmade leather bags—complemented by Marion Heilig's micro-fine gold bangles and Joachim Dombrowski's pearl creations. *Tucholskystrasse 31.* ☎ *030-282-11-52. www.penthesileia.de. AE, MC, V. S-Bahn: Oranienburger Strasse. Map p 86.*

★★★ **Tausche** PRENZLAUER BERG Tausche's groovy shoulder bags are waterproof and durable. The fun comes in choosing your flap—with 100 designs, your bag can sport a different one for every day of the week. *Raumerstrasse 8.* ☎ *030-40-30-17-70. www.tausche-berlin.de. AE, MC, V. U-Bahn: Eberswalder Strasse. Map p 86.*

★ **Thatchers** MITTE Homegrown fashion gurus Ralf Hensellek and Thomas Mrozek design sassy, versatile clothes for young urbanites. From slinky clubwear to shift dresses and stoles, their clothing is sexy yet understated. *Hackesche Höfe.* ☎ *030-27-58-22-10. www.thatchers.de. AE, MC, V. S-Bahn: Hackescher Markt. Map p 86.*

★ **Waahnsinn** MITTE This eccentric store stocks an array of vintage, new fashion, and gifts. Find oversized 1960s shades, miniature Fernsehturms, beaded ball gowns, retro lamps, and strapping lederhosen. *Rosenthaler Strasse 17.* ☎ *030-282-00-29. www.waahnsinn-berlin.de. MC, V. U-Bahn: Rosenthaler Platz. Map p 86.*

Food Specialists

★★ **Absinth Depot** MITTE Nicknamed the "green fairy," absinthe was the preferred tipple in bohemian haunts of fin-de-siècle Paris. This delightfully old-world shop-cum-bar stocks 130 absinthe varieties and flavors. *Weinmeisterstrasse 4.* ☎ *030-281-67-89. V. U-Bahn: Weinmeisterstrasse. Map p 86.*

★★ kids **Bonbonmacherei** MITTE An aroma of peppermint fills the air at this candy store. Sweet treats, from sour limes to the famous leaf-shaped *Maiblätter* (May leaves) with woodruff are made by hand here. *Heckmannhöfe, Oranienburger Strasse 32.* ☎ *030-44-05-52-43. No credit cards. S-Bahn: Oranienburger Strasse. Map p 86.*

Vibrant hats on display at Penthesileia.

The walls of Tausche are lined with colorful bag flaps.

★★ Confiserie Mélanie CHARLOTTENBURG   Indulge your sweet tooth at this charmingly old-fashioned confectionary store. Find truffles made with unusual ingredients like garlic, horseradish, curry, lavender, and porcini-olive. *Goethestrasse 4.* ☎ *030-313-83-30. www.bei-melanie.de. MC, V. S.Bahn: Savignyplatz. Map p 85.*

★ kids Kadó KREUZBERG   Licorice lovers should make for this old-world store, where glass jars brim with organic laces, salty Dutch-style dragees, and drops with ginger, aniseed, and violet. The licorice here is just right: chewy and not too sweet. *Gräfestrasse 20.* ☎ *030-69-04-16-38. No credit cards. U-Bahn: Schönleinstrasse. Map p 86.*

★★ kids Königsberger Marzipan CHARLOTTENBURG   You can tell you're in for a treat the moment you enter this family-run store. Marzipan is made the old-fashioned way and then lovingly hand-wrapped. *Pestalozzistrasse 54a.* ☎ *030-323-82-54. No credit cards. U-Bahn: Wilmersdorfer Strasse. Map p 85.*

★ kids Leysieffer CHARLOTTENBURG   Since 1909, this confectioner's has sold handmade chocolate, preserves, gingerbread, and melt-in-the-mouth truffles. I love unusual chocolate varieties like sea-salt, chili, sloe berry, and Indian spices. *Kurfürstendamm 218.* ☎ *030-885-74-80. AE, MC, V. U-Bahn: Uhlandstrasse. Map p 85.*

★ Pesto Dealer CHARLOTTENBERG   Wild garlic and rocket, cashew and Thai: This deli reaches new dimensions with its fresh homemade pesto. It's also the go-to shop for quality Italian wines, pasta, olive oil, and balsamic vinegar. *Goethestrasse 34.* ☎ *017-85-59-85-10. No credit cards. U-Bahn: Wilmersdorfer Strasse. Map p 85.*

★ Sagers CHARLOTTENBERG   Award-winning, freshly roasted coffee that smells and tastes divine. Espresso, fair-trade, and organic coffees are roasted from Arabica beans to achieve an irresistible aroma. *Lotte-Lenya-Bogen 555.* ☎ *017-26-25-61-59. No credit cards. S-Bahn: Zoologischer Garten. Map p 85.*

★ Senf Salon KREUZBERG   Homemade varieties of mustard flavored with lavender, banana, chili, fig, beer, or red garlic share shelf-space with chutneys and marmalades at this basement store. You can try before you buy. *Hagelberger Strasse 46.* ☎ *030-78-89-11-01. www.senfsalon.de. AE, MC, V. U-Bahn: Mehringdamm. Map p 86.*

Spazio Feinkost KREUZBERG   Planning a picnic in Viktoriapark? You can fill your basket with the best of Italian hams, cheeses, crostini, salami, and olives at this friendly deli. They also do a fine line in Italian wine and Prosecco. *Kreuzbergstrasse 15.* ☎ *030-81-82-87-50. No credit cards. U-Bahn: Mehringdamm. Map p 86.*

★ **Teeladen** MITTE Take in the scent of herbal infusions at this hole-in-the-wall tea shop. Fine brews sold by the gram range from classics like green and breakfast tea to more unusual varieties like caramel and pink grapefruit. *Propststrasse 3.* ☎ *030-242-32-55. AE, DC, MC, V. U-Bahn: Klosterstrasse. Map p 86.*

Gifts

★ **Ach Berlin** MITTE Pop into this Gendarmenmarkt for unique souvenirs. T-shirts printed with city landmarks, USB sticks shaped like the Fernsehturm, retro bags, and skyline keyrings—you'll find plenty of gift inspiration here. *Alte Markgrafenstrasse 39.* ☎ *030-92-12-68-80. MC, V. U-Bahn: Hausvogteiplatz. Map p 86.*

★★ **Ampelmann** MITTE This Hackesche Höfe store pays tribute to East Germany's much-loved *Ampelmännchen*. Emblazoned with the red or green traffic light man, its retro lamps, T-shirts, umbrellas, and bags make original gifts. *Hof V, Hackesche Höfe.* ☎ *030-44-72-64-38. www.ampelmann.de. MC, V. S-Bahn: Hackescher Markt. Map p 86.*

Ampelmann gallery shop.

★ **Erzgebirgshaus** MITTE It's forever Christmas at this traditional store selling hand-carved wooden decorations from the Erzgebirge, in Saxony. Pick up nutcrackers, incense-smoking carved figures, and candelabras. *Friedrichstrasse 194–199.* ☎ *030-20-45-09-77. AE, MC, V. U-Bahn: Stadtmitte. Map p 86.*

kids **Keramik Selber Bemahlen** KREUZBERG Release your inner Van Gogh at this paint-it-yourself ceramics shop. Pick your pottery (from olive dishes to egg cups) and get colorful with brushes and 60 shades of paint. *Mehringdamm 73/cnr Bergmannstrasse.* ☎ *030-28-83-73-55. www. paintyourstyle.de. MC, V. U-Bahn: Mehringdamm. Map p 86.*

★ **Koko von Knebel** CHARLOTTENBURG An eccentric doggy world for pampered pooches. Designer Udo Waltz has created a line of canine clothing including gem-encrusted collars (from punk to Playboy bunny), raincoats, and even lingerie. *Uhlandstrasse 181.* ☎ *043-19-97-08-68. AE, MC, V. U-Bahn: Uhlandstrasse. Map p 85.*

★ **Kwik Shop** PRENZLAUER BERG The enterprising owners of this quirky kiosk have trawled the world for oddities from Breton mussel baskets and brightly colored Wellington boots to sausage-dog doorstops. *Kastanienallee 44.* ☎ *030-41-99-71-50. MC, V. U-Bahn: Rosa-Luxemburg-Platz. Map p 86.*

★ **Lomography Gallery Store** MITTE This store is an ode to the cult Russian camera. Get stocked up with everything from Lomo fisheye and panoramic cameras to accessories to achieve weird and wonderful photographic effects. *Friedrichstrasse 133.* ☎ *030-20-21-51-62. U-Bahn: Friedrichstrasse. Map p 86.*

Jewelry & Accessories
Buckles & Belts MITTE   This glam store turns buckles and Italian leather belts into an art form. The mind-boggling buckle range stretches from one-of-a-kind artists' creations to those inspired by natural motifs. *Alte Schonhauserstrasse 14.* ☎ *030-28-09-30-70. AE, DC, MC, V. U-Bahn: Rosa-Luxemburg-Platz. Map p 86.*

★★ **Gallery Schrill** CHARLOTTEN-BURG   This girly boudoir is well-stocked with tiaras, vintage brooches, and pearls the size of plums. Out back are original works by German artist Elvira Bach. Gents will find an outstanding cufflink collection. *Bleibtreustrasse 48.* ☎ *030-882-33-66. www.schrill.de. AE, MC, V. S-Bahn: Savignyplatz. Map p 85.*

★ **Glanzstücke** MITTE   Bejeweled evening bags, feather boas, and Art Deco dragonfly brooches—this Hackesche Höfe boutique glitters with 20th-century costume jewelry for well-dressed divas. *Hackesche Höfe.* ☎ *030-208-26-76. AE, MC, V. S-Bahn: Hackescher Markt. Map p 86.*

Vintage costume jewelery sparkles at Gallery Schrill.

Music
Da Capo PRENZLAUER BERG   This musty record store has an eclectic mix of vinyl. Flick through rock, reggae grooves, jazz, classical, and GDR labels. The interior is a flash-back to the Swinging Sixties. *Kastanienallee 96.* ☎ *030-448-17-71. No credit cards. U-Bahn: Eberswalder Strasse. Map p 86.*

Dussmann MITTE   Open till mid-night, this megastore is packed with

Berlin's Markets

When the sun's out, Berlin's markets beckon. In Prenzlauer Berg, **Ökomarkt Kollwitzplatz** (Thurs noon–7pm, Sat 9am–4pm) has stalls piled high with locally sourced, organic produce from wholemeal breads to cheese and flowers. True bargains are rare, but it's still fun to wander around the **flea market** along Strasse des 17 Juni (Sat and Sun 10am–5pm) for collectables and crafts from fancy hats to gramophones. Kreuzberg's canalside **Turkish Market** along Maybachufer (Tues and Fri 11am–6:30pm) offers up garlicky olives, spices, and glossy eggplants. Pause to munch on a kebab between purchases.

Antiques and bric-a-brac at the weekend flea market on Strasse des 17 Juni.

books, films, and CDs. The entire musical spectrum is covered, although it is known best for having the largest classical music department in the world. *Friedrichstrasse 90.* ☎ *030-20-25-11-11. AE, MC, V. U-Bahn: Französische Strasse. Map p 86.*

Space Hall KREUZBERG   The music skips from electro and house to retro and techno at this funky Kreuzberg store, with a huge variety of CDs old and new. The friendly staff will help you find what you're looking for. *Zossener Strasse 33.* ☎ *030-694-76-64. AE, MC, V. U-Bahn: Gneisenaustrasse. Map p 86.*

Shoes

Budapester Schuhe CHAR-LOTTENBURG   Smart-dressed gents should invest in a pair of these high-quality, soft-leather shoes. The craftsmanship is top-notch and the styles, many of them Italian, are timeless. It's worth looking out for sale items. *Kurfürstendamm 43.* ☎ *030-88-62-42-06. AE, DC, MC, V. U-Bahn: Uhlandstrasse. Map p 85.*

kids Camper CHARLOTTEN-BURG   This poster-plastered store is the Berlin outpost of Spain's funkiest footwear store, with a huge array of shoes and sneakers for adults and kids. Best of all, the bright, poster-plastered walls can be ripped to reveal geometric designs. *Kurfürstendamm 26a.* ☎ *030-88-71-44-53. AE, MC, V. U-Bahn: Uhlandstrasse. Map p 85.*

flip*flop® Concept Store MITTE   This cool store sells footwear designed to avoid a poolside fashion *faux pas*. Find sandals, pumps, boots, and accessories for the sexiest feet on the strand or in

the snow. *Alte Schönhauser Strasse 41.* ☎ *030-20-05-42-95. www.flip-flop.de. MC, V. U-Bahn: Weinmeister-strasse. Map p 86.*

Toys

★★ **kids Barefoot Berlin** KREUZ-BERG   Kids love Barefoot's fair-trade toys, handwoven from natural materials in Sri Lanka. The rainbow-colored octopuses, reversible armadillos, and kangaroo backpacks are child magnets. *Kreuzbergstrasse 75.* ☎ *030-39-20-70-46. AE, MC, V. U-Bahn: Mehringdamm. Map p 86.*

Fair-trade toys at Barefoot Berlin.

★ **kids Katalka** PRENZLAUER BERG   Chunky wooden toys, many hand-made, fill this colorful store in "baby boom" district Prenzlauer Berg. Beside trikes, building blocks, and pirate ships are dolls house figurines, puppets, and much more. *Raumerstrasse 21.* ☎ *030-49-85-33-77. MC, V. U-Bahn: Eberswalder Strasse. Map p 86.*

★ **Ratzekatz** PRENZLAUER BERG   This toy wonderland brims with high-quality playthings from kites to board games, building blocks, coloring materials, jigsaws, and plush animals. It also has a superb array of hand puppets to spark little imaginations. *Raumerstrasse 7.* ☎ *030-681-95-64. MC, V. U-Bahn: Eberswalder Strasse. Map p 86.*

kids Steiff CHARLOTTEN-BURG   Steiff's classic teddy is jointed, plush, and comes with an ear tag. His furry friends include polar bears, huskies, and grizzlies. Though not cheap, these cuddly toys are made to last. *Kurfürstendamm 220.* ☎ *030-88-62-51-58. AE, MC, V. U-Bahn: Kurfürstendamm. Map p 85.* ●

Tiergarten

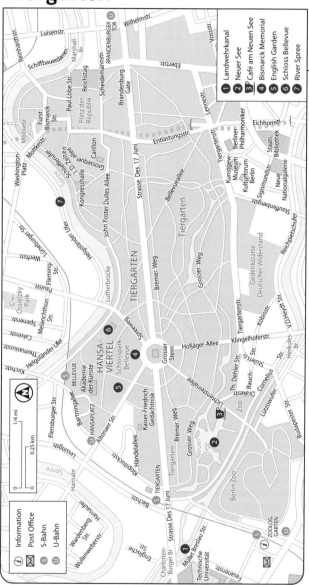

1 Landwehrkanal
2 Neuer See
3 Cafe am Neuen See
4 Bismarck Memorial
5 English Garden
6 Schloss Bellevue
7 River Spree

Previous page: Chinese Tea House, Marzahn Gardens.

Berlin's biggest outdoor playground is a vast swathe of greenery studded with lakes and canals. You'll find some quiet corners, but most of Tiergarten hums with activity, from picnicking families to rollerblading teenagers. Footpaths weave through these woodlands where Prussian princes once went hunting, affording snapshot glimpses of the Siegessäule. START: **S-Bahn to Tiergarten.**

① ★★ kids Landwehrkanal.
Begin your stroll on the grassy banks of Berlin's main canal, the Landwehrkanal. Shadowing the water, the tree-fringed Gartenufer skirts the zoo (p 26), and offers a sneak preview. Peek through the fence to spy hyenas, storks, and llamas. Cross the bridge to reach the serene rose gardens. ⏱ *30 min. S-Bahn: Tiergarten.*

② ★ kids Neuer See. A few paces away is the lake, mirroring a copse of oak, ash, and maple. When the sun's out, the best way to appreciate it is by hiring a rowing boat (5€ for 30 minutes). ⏱ *45 min. See p 20.*

③ ★ kids Café am Neuen See.
Beautifully situated by the lake, this cafe is a terrific spot to enjoy a cold beer or ice cream, and soak up the views of Tiergarten. *Lichtensteinallee 2.* ☎ *030-254-49-30.* €–€€.

④ Bismarck Memorial. Ambling north along Altonaer Strasse, you'll be drawn to this striking memorial to Otto von Bismarck, Prime Minister of Prussia (1862–83) and the first Chancellor of Germany (1871–90),

famous for creating and shaping the modern German state. Immortalized in bronze, he lords it over a globe-bearing statue of Atlas. ⏱ *20 min.*

⑤ ★ English Garden. This landscaped English garden in the heart of Tiergarten is a calm haven where fountains gurgle beside neatly clipped bushes, flowerbeds, and a central sundial. If you're here in July or August, don't miss the **Konzertsommer** (*www.konzertsommer.info*) for free jazz and world music concerts on the weekends. ⏱ *30 min.*

⑥ ★ Schloss Bellevue. Edging slightly north brings you to the manicured gardens surrounding the neo-classical Schloss Bellevue. Tucked behind the palace is the Bellevue Ufer promenade where locals come to laze on the sun-dappled banks of the river. ⏱ *30 min. See p 13.*

⑦ ★★ River Spree. From here, I like to trace the meandering Spree east along Helgoländer Ufer. The promenade provides a wonderful transition from Charlottenburg to Mitte as the greenery fades and the landmarks of Berlin's cityscape gradually unfold. ⏱ *45 min.*

The River Spree.

Wannsee & Around

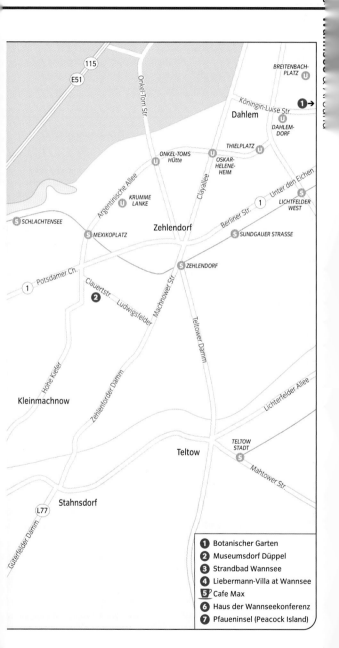

1 Botanischer Garten
2 Museumsdorf Düppel
3 Strandbad Wannsee
4 Liebermann-Villa at Wannsee
5 Cafe Max
6 Haus der Wannseekonferenz
7 Pfaueninsel (Peacock Island)

As the German ditty goes, when the sun shines it's time to Pack die Badehose ein (pack your bathing trunks) and jump on the train to Wannsee. Kick back in a wicker lounger and feel the sand between your toes. Alternatively, spend a day exploring the nearby botanical gardens, painter Max Liebermann's villa, and the whimsical palace of King Friedrich Wilhelm II. START: **S-Bahn to Botanischer Garten.**

➊ ★★ Botanischer Garten.

Berlin's sublime botanical garden is among the world's largest, with around 22,000 plant species. Stroll the tropical greenhouses full of orchids, azaleas, and oddities such as the South African Welwitschia (a living fossil), Lithops (flowering stones), and the magnificent Victoria, a giant water lily that flowers every summer. I love the sweet-scented sensory garden, particularly when it's ablaze with spring flowers. Another must is the plant geography section to wander past different types of vegetation that grows in the Northern Hemisphere. It nurtures everything from European beech forest to alpine flowers. ⏰ *1 hr. Königin-Luise-Strasse 6–8.* ☎ *030-83-85-01-00. www.botanischer-garten-berlin.de. Admission 6€ adults, 3€ concessions, free for children under 6. Daily summer 9am–9pm; winter 9am–4pm. S-Bahn: Botanischer Garten.*

Greenhouse at the Botanischer Garten.

➋ ★ kids Museumsdorf Düppel.

Tie in your visit with a trip to this reconstructed medieval village complete with thatched cottages, herb gardens, and stalls for oxen and sheep. Kids can also learn about traditional crafts such as pottery and basket weaving. It's officially in German, but staff may speak a little English. ⏰ *1 hr. Clauertstrasse 11.* ☎ *030-802-66-71. www.dueppel.de. Admission 2€ adults, 1€ children. Apr–Sept Thurs 3–7pm, Sun 10am–5pm. S-Bahn: Zehlendorf.*

➌ ★★★ kids Strandbad Wannsee.

Just a short trundle from central Berlin, Wannsee is the favorite summertime playground of Berliners seeking sun, sand, and the next best thing to the sea. A 10-minute walk through pine forest from S-Bahn Nikolassee brings you to the beachfront bathing complex, lined

with *Strandkörbe*, snazzy basket-like reclining beach chairs. Veer left of the jetty and you find a playground, volleyball court, and pedalo rental. Over to the right lies the FKK (nudist beach), for those who dare to bare all. Stay after the crowds leave to watch the sun set. ⏱ *1 hr. Wannseebadweg 25.* ☎ *030-803-54-50. Admission 4€ adults, 2.50€ children. May–Aug Mon–Fri 10am–7pm, Sat–Sun 8am–8pm; Sept daily 10am–7pm. S-Bahn: Nikolassee.*

❹ ★★ **Liebermann-Villa at Wannsee.** A meander along the lakefront brings you to the pink summer villa of Max Liebermann (1847–1935), affectionately dubbed by the artist as his "castle by the sea." Behind a neoclassical facade, art lovers are treated to an exquisite collection of his Impressionist pastels, prints, and paintings, most inspired by Wannsee and the gardens surrounding the villa. These have been lovingly recreated to their former glory with groomed lawns and red geraniums. ⏱ *45 min. Colomierstrasse 3.* ☎ *030-80-58-59-00. www.max-liebermann.de. Admission 6€ adults, 4€ concessions, free for children under 14. Apr–Oct Wed–Mon 10am–6pm; Nov–Mar Wed–Mon 11am–5pm. S-Bahn: Wannsee.*

🄺 **Cafe Max.** Set in the elegant Liebermann family dining room, the museum cafe is a fine spot for afternoon coffee or a light snack. Sit on the lake-facing terrace when the sun shines. *Colomierstrasse 3.* ☎ *030-80-49-84-33. €.*

❻ ★★ **Haus der Wannseekonferenz.** Farther west along the waterfront you reach another mansion, dating from 1914, whose cream stone exterior belies a sobering past. In 1942, Reinhard Heydrich and other senior SS officers convened

Relax in a Strandkorb *at Strandbad Wannsee.*

here for the Wannsee Conference, where they plotted the Final Solution to annihilate Europe's Jews. A simple, moving exhibition commemorates Holocaust victims. ⏱ *45 min. Am Grossen Wannsee 56–58.* ☎ *030-308-05-00-10. www.ghwk.de. Admission free. Daily 10am–6pm. S-Bahn: Wannsee.*

❼ ★★★ **Pfaueninsel (Peacock Island).** This UNESCO World Heritage site epitomizes Prussian pomp and romantic folly. Designed by King Friedrich Wilhelm II in 1793, the 67 hectare (165 acre) garden is wooded with ancient oaks. First up when you step off the ferry is the Schloss, a miniature castle sporting mock ruins. It was here that Friedrich used to flock with his beloved Wilhelmine. Amble slightly north to the aviary inhabited by the island's namesake peacocks and at the northernmost tip lies the neo-Gothic Meierei, built to resemble a ruined monastery. *Frequent ferry from Nikolskoer Weg 2€ adults, 1€ children. Daily summer 8am–9pm; winter 10am–4pm. S-Bahn: Wannsee.*

Marzahn **Gardens**

1. Oriental Garden
2. Fountain & Spring Garden
3. Maze & Labyrinth
4. Italian Renaissance Garden
5. Chinese Garden
6. Chinese Tea House
7. Playground
8. Japanese Garden
9. Korean Garden
10. Balinese Garden

Tucked between the prefabricated housing estates in the socially deprived suburb of Marzahn-Hellersdorf, these enchanting gardens come as a surprise. The so-called Gardens of the World are botanical globetrotting at its best, taking you from Bali's tropical lushness to the quiet simplicity of a Japanese rock garden. Allow at least half a day to see this urban oasis. START: **S-Bahn to Marzahn.**

1 ★ **Oriental Garden.** Moroccan garden historian Mohammed El Fai'z and Algerian landscape architect Kamel Louafi pooled their knowledge to design this green retreat, nurturing fruit trees, roses, and exotic plants. Enclosed by a high wall, the garden embodies the key principles of Islamic garden design: geometry, shade, and water. ⏱ *20 min.*

2 ★ **Fountain & Spring Garden.** The sound of water trickling from boulders, pebbles, and millstones creates a soothing ambiance in this garden. Follow the zigzagging path past 14 fountains that dance against a verdant backdrop of bamboo and pampas grass. The garden is a calm space that brings together the elements of earth and water. ⏱ *15 min.*

3 ★★ **kids Maze & Labyrinth.** Be prepared to get lost within the bewildering maze and labyrinth. This clever juxtaposition shows how the two differ: A labyrinth has only one route to the center, whereas a maze presents multiple options. High enough to prevent peeking, the yew hedge maze is modeled on Hampton Court, outside London. Scale the tower by the gingko tree to plot your route. The mosaic labyrinth next door is inspired by that of the Gothic cathedral in Chartres, France; a light-gray pebble path leads to its center, which is marked by a circular pool that represents a "heavenly mirror." ⏱ *40 min.*

4 ★ **Italian Renaissance Garden.** Designed for the appreciation

Detail of the flame-red pagoda in Marzahn's Chinese Garden.

of nature, Italian Renaissance gardens were often symmetrical in form and adorned with mythological statues. This garden is a fine example, with its clipped box hedges, central fountain, and plants in terracotta pots. Look out for the marble statue of Bobolina, a replica of the 16th-century original in the Boboli Gardens, Florence. ⏱ *25 min.*

5 ★★★ **Chinese Garden.** The highlight of a trip to Marzahn is Europe's largest Chinese garden. Pass the stone lions and enter the circular moon gate for flame-red pagodas and pavilions, gushing fountains, and covered bridges with lattice windows that frame the view. It's as close as you can get to Beijing's Summer Palace without setting foot outside Berlin. A mosaic path twists past willows, maples,

Practical Matters

Marzahn is a short trek from the center. Take the S-Bahn to Marzahn, and then a 5-minute ride on bus 195 from the stand opposite the station, which drops you off at the gate. Entry costs 3€ (half price for children under 14). Opening hours are daily from 9am to dusk, but some of the gardens (for instance Korea and Japan) close earlier. For further details, call ☎ 030-546-98-12 or see www.gaerten-der-welt.de.

and bamboo to a lake dotted with lotus flowers. ⏱ *1 hr.*

6 ★★ **Chinese Tea House.** This curve-roofed pagoda is the centerpiece of the Chinese garden. Ladies in traditional costume bear trays laden with *baozi* (sweet dumplings) and pots of aromatic chrysanthemum and jade tea. *Chinese Garden.* ☎ 017-93-94-55-64. €.

7 kids **Playground.** Exit China and pass the Confucius statue to reach this playground, where kids can play freely in green surrounds. Tire swings, climbing frames, hanging bridges, and two giant bears keep them amused. ⏱ *15 min.*

8 ★★ **Japanese Garden.** This meticulously landscaped example of Japanese garden design remains faithful to Zen principles. Flowering dogwoods, lavender, orchids, and sloe berries create a stark contrast with stylistic elements such as dry streams and artfully raked gravel in the *karesansui* (Japanese rock garden). I like to come in spring, when it's a swathe of pink cherry blossom. ⏱ *30 min.*

9 ★★ **Korean Garden.** *Jangseung* totem poles (said to ward off evil spirits) give you a toothy grin at the entrance to the Korean Garden. Inside, discover a quiet haven for contemplation, sheltering courtyards, and rockeries that emphasize Taoist principles of mystery and discovering nature. The layout is typical of the Korean tradition, with a pavilion perched above a clear stream supposed to highlight the pleasure of watching water. ⏱ *20 min.*

Jangseung totem poles at Marzahn's Korean Garden.

10 ★★ **Balinese Garden.** Positively steamy in winter, this tropical glasshouse showcases native Balinese flora. The garden reflects the Balinese philosophy of harmony through plants that are functional as well as attractive, providing food, medicine, or shade. A path leads past fern palms and crotons, moon orchids, and the sweet-scented flowers of the frangipani tree. Even on a cold, miserable day, whiffs of incense and ambient music evoke Indonesia. ⏱ *20 min.* ●

Dining Best Bets

Look for the sign at Curry 36, home to Berlin's legendary Currywurst (curried sausage).

Best **Falafel**
★★ Dada Falafel *Linienstrasse 132* (p 33)

Best **Riverside Dining**
★★★ Patio *Helgoländer Ufer/ Kirchstrasse (p 115)*

Best **Michelin Star Splurge**
★★★ Vau *Jägerstrasse 54 (p 116)*

Best **Skyline Views**
★★★ Solar *Stresemannstrasse 76* (p 116)

Best for **Families**
★★ Ampelmann Restaurant *Stadtbahnbogen 159/160 (p 111)*

Best **Spicy Sausage**
★★ Curry 36 *Mehringdamm 36* (p 16)

Best for **Chocolate Indulgence**
★ Fassbender & Rausch *Charlottenstrasse 60 (p 112)*

Best **Alpine Flavors**
★★ Schneeweiss *Simplonstrasse 16* (p 116)

Best **Old-World Tavern**
★★ Gasthaus Krombach *Meinekestrasse 4 (p 113)*

Best **Gourmet Vegetarian**
★★★ Cookies Cream *Friedrichstrasse 158 (p 112)*

Best **California-Style Snacks**
Dolores *Rosa-Luxemburg-Strasse 7* (p 112)

Best **Authentic Anatolian**
★ Mey *Bleibtreustrasse 47 (p 114)*

Best **French Brasserie**
★★ Entrecôte *Schützenstrasse 5* (p 112)

Best **Budget**
★ Henne *Leuschnerdamm 25 (p 113)*

Best **Austrian Fare**
★ Riehmer's *Hagelbergerstrasse 9* (p 115)

Best **Berlin Soul Food**
★ Marjellchen *Mommsenstrasse 9* (p 113)

Best **Pizza in Town**
★ Il Casolare *Grimmstrasse 30 (p 113)*

Best **Black Forest Flavors**
★ Schwarzwaldstuben *Tucholskystrasse 48 (p 116)*

Best **Tapas Bar**
★ Tafelgold *Niederbarnimstrasse 11* (p 116)

Best **Pan-Asian**
★ Nu *Schlüterstrasse 55 (p 115)*

Best for **Culinary Adventures**
★★ Jules Verne *Schlüterstrasse 61* (p 113)

Best **Swabian Specialties**
★ Maultaschen Manufaktur *Lützowstrasse 22 (p 114)*

Best **Italian**
★★ Vino e Libri *Torstrasse 99* (p 116)

Previous page: NU Restaurant.

Charlottenburg **Dining**

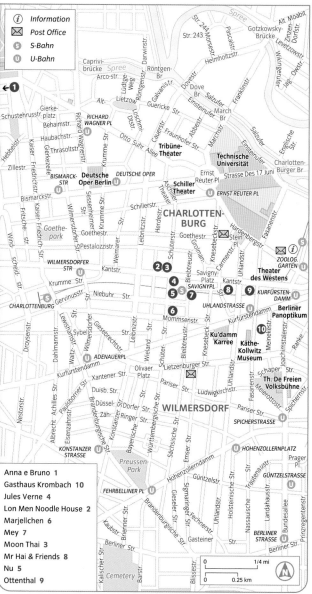

Anna e Bruno 1
Gasthaus Krombach 10
Jules Verne 4
Lon Men Noodle House 2
Marjellchen 6
Mey 7
Moon Thai 3
Mr Hai & Friends 8
Nu 5
Ottenthal 9

The Best Dining

Mitte & Prenzlauer Berg **Dining**

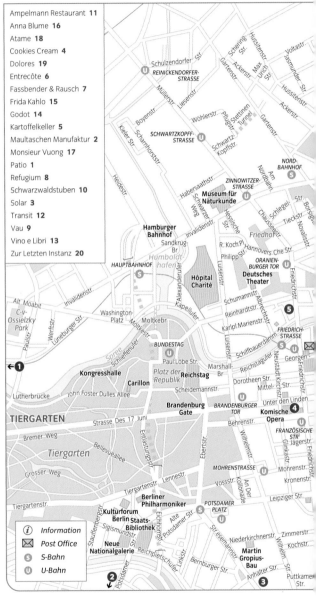

ⓘ Information
✉ Post Office
Ⓢ S-Bahn
Ⓤ U-Bahn

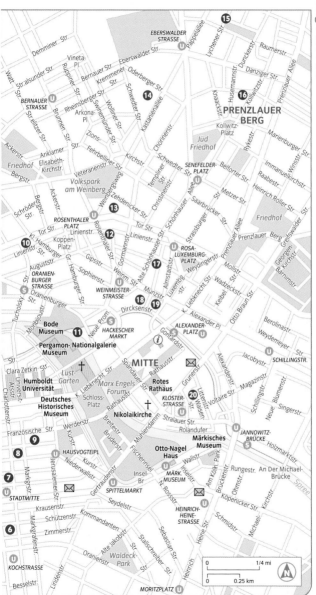

Kreuzberg & Friedrichshain **Dining**

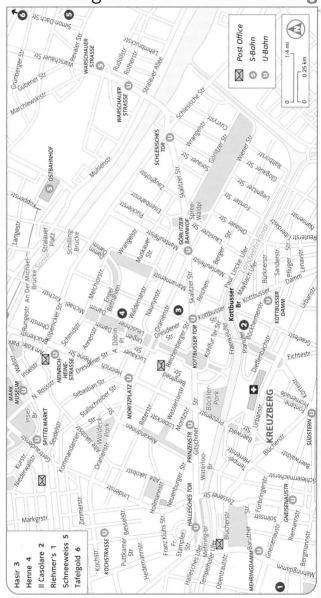

Post Office

S-Bahn

U-Bahn

Hasir 3
Henne 4
Il Casolare 2
Riehmer's 1
Schneeweiss 5
Tafelgold 6

Dining A to Z

★★ kids Ampelmann Restaurant MITTE *ITALIAN* Under the S-Bahn arches, this bistro pays homage to Berlin's legendary traffic light man. The wood-fired pizzas are large and tasty, or go for spot-on Italian entrees like risotto with artichokes, rocket, and sundried tomatoes. *Stadtbahnbogen 159/160.* ☎ *030-84-71-07-09. www.ampelmann-restaurant.de. Entrees 7.50€–17.50€. MC, V. Lunch and dinner daily. S-Bahn: Hackescher Markt. Map p 108.*

★ kids Anna Blume PRENZLAUER BERG *DESSERTS* Named after Kurt Schwitters' romantic poem, this bijou cafe-cum-florist always tempts me with moist poppy cake and Chinese rose tea. The terrace is a fine spot for people-watching amid the blooms. *Kollwitzstrasse 83.* ☎ *030-44-04-87-49. Snacks 3.50€–8€. No credit cards. Breakfast, lunch, and dinner daily. U-Bahn: Eberswalder Strasse. Map p 108.*

★ Anna e Bruno CHARLOTTEN-BURG *ITALIAN* Chef Bruno Pellegrini puts a modern spin on Italian cuisine at this avant-garde restaurant. Dress up to join smart diners for signature dishes such as octopus carpaccio with saffron fennel and chocolate lasagna with kumquats. Reservations recommended. *Sophie-Charlotten-Strasse 101.* ☎ *030-325-71-10. Entrees 25€–35€. MC, V. Dinner daily. S-Bahn: Westend. Map p 107.*

Atame MITTE *TAPAS* Chilies hang above the bar at this high-ceilinged tapas haunt, where the walls are plastered with posters of Almodóvar films. Savor a glass of Rioja and tasty Spanish morsels such as *boquerones* (sardines) and garlicky prawns. *Dircksenstrasse 40.* ☎ *030-28-04-25-60. Tapas 2€–8€. MC, V. Lunch and dinner daily. S-Bahn: Hackescher Markt. Map p 108.*

Ampelmann Restaurant.

★★★ **Cookies Cream** MITTE *VEG-ETARIAN* Shoehorned down a dark alley behind the Westin Grand, this über-trendy restaurant sports an industrial-chic interior and serves gourmet vegetarian cuisine. Try lentil strudel, pumpkin gnocchi, and chocolate-rosemary fondant with milk-sherbet ice cream. *Friedrichstrasse 158.* ☎ *030-27-49-29-40. 3-course menu 32€. MC, V. Dinner Tues–Sat. U-Bahn: Französische Strasse. Map p 108.*

Dolores MITTE *CALIFORNIAN* As bright, young, and effortlessly hip as an L.A. diner, Dolores dishes up Californian-style fare, with plenty of choice for vegans. Pick side dishes and salsas to accompany tasty mains like burritos and quesadillas. *Rosa-Luxemburg-Strasse 7.* ☎ *030-28-04-25-60. www.dolores-berlin.de. Entrees 4€–7€. MC, V. Lunch and dinner daily. S-Bahn: Rosa-Luxemburg-Platz. Map p 108.*

★★ **Entrecôte** MITTE *FRENCH* With its banquette seating, bustling ambiance, and efficient service, this high-ceilinged brasserie captures the spirit of Paris. The typical French menu includes steak minute with frites and escargots. *Schützenstrasse 5.* ☎ *030-20-16-54-96. Entrees 12€–26€. MC, V. Lunch Mon–Fri, dinner Mon–Sat. U-Bahn: Stadtmitte. Map p 108.*

★ **Fassbender & Rausch** MITTE *CHOCOLATE* Europe's first chocolate restaurant is sinfully sweet and waistline-expanding. The famed chocolatiers have channeled their cocoa know-how into dishes such as Tobago chocolate cannelloni and fresh shrimp pasta in lemon-chocolate butter. *Charlottenstrasse 60.* ☎ *030-20-45-84-43. Entrees 19€–23€. MC, V. Lunch and dinner daily. U-Bahn: Stadtmitte. Map p 108.*

★ **Frida Kahlo** PRENZLAUER BERG *MEXICAN* As vibrant as Kahlo's paintings, this dazzling blue Mexican *pulqueria* rolls out tasty fajitas and nachos, and is famous for its lazy brunches. *Lychener Strasse 37.* ☎ *030-445-70-16. www.fridakahlo. de. Entrees 8€–15€. MC, V. Lunch and dinner daily. U-Bahn: Eberswalder Strasse. Map p 108.*

Californian-style restaurant Dolores.

★★ **Gasthaus Krombach** CHAR-LOTTENBURG *GERMAN* It can be hard to find proper old-fashioned Berlin cuisine, but this softly lit wood-paneled tavern hits the mark. Classics like *Eisbein* (pork knuckles) and *Königsberger Klopse* (Prussian meatballs in white wine sauce) are the stars of the rich, hearty menu. *Meinekestrasse 4.* ☎ *030-881-86-02. www.gasthaus-krombach.de. Entrees 8€–15€. MC, V. Lunch and dinner daily. U-Bahn: Uhlandstrasse. Map p 107.*

Godot PRENZLAUER BERG *BRUNCH* Berlin's hipsters gather on the ivy-draped courtyard of this boho cafe for a baguette (served with thick-cut vegetables) and an espresso. Candles, exposed brickwork, and a comic-plastered ceiling give it a relaxed, shabby-chic feel. *Kastanienallee 16–17.* ☎ *030-54-71-36-59. Snacks 2€–7€. No credit cards. Breakfast, lunch, and dinner daily. U-Bahn: Eberswalder Strasse. Map p 108.*

★ kids **Hasir** KREUZBERG *TURKISH* This family-run Turkish outpost has been spicing up Kreuzberg since 1971. Aromatic specialties include warm flat bread, lamb shish kebabs, and tempting syrup sweets. *Adalbertstrasse 10.* ☎ *030-614-23-73. Entrees 11.50€–19€. No credit cards. Lunch and dinner daily. U-Bahn: Kottbusser Tor. Map p 110.*

★★ **Henne** KREUZBERG *GERMAN* There's one prerequisite for visiting Henne: You gotta like chicken, because that's all there is. Crispy corn-fed poultry lands on your plate with lashings of coleslaw and potatoes. Reservations are essential. *Leuschnerdamm 25.* ☎ *030-614-77-30. Entrees 6€–8€. MC, V. Dinner Tues–Sun. U-Bahn: Moritzplatz. Map p 110.*

★ kids **Il Casolare** KREUZBERG *PIZZA* The service may be indifferent, but for authentic wood-fired pizza, it's hard to beat Il Casolare. This canal-side pizzeria is always packed, so reservations are a must. *Grimmstrasse 30.* ☎ *030-69-50-66-10. Entrees 5€–12€. No credit cards. Lunch and dinner daily. U-Bahn: Schönleinstrasse. Map p 110.*

★★ **Jules Verne** CHARLOTTENBURG *FRENCH* This intimate, candlelit bistro, discreetly peppered with Jules Verne memorabilia, offers superb weekend brunches along with French classics such as oysters or juicy rump steaks with pommes frites. *Schlüterstrasse 61.* ☎ *030-31-80-94-10. www.jules-verne-berlin.de. Entrees 10.50€–24€. MC, V. Breakfast, lunch, and dinner daily. S-Bahn: Savignyplatz. Map p 107.*

Kartoffelkeller MITTE *GERMAN* Venture down to these cozy vaults to pick from a huge range of spud-inspired dishes. The potato-packed menu reaches from herby pancakes to Swiss rösti. There's a beer garden in summer. *Albrechtstrasse 14b.* ☎ *030-282-85-48. Entrees 7€–14€. MC, V. Lunch and dinner daily. S-Bahn: Friedrichstrasse. Map p 108.*

Lon Men Noodle House CHARLOTTENBURG *TAIWANESE* The spicy noodle soups, prawn dim sum, and rice noodles here are all great value. If you're feeling adventurous, try a side order of crispy pig's ears. *Kantstrasse 33.* ☎ *030-31-51-96-78. Entrees 5€–7€. No credit cards. Lunch and dinner daily. S-Bahn: Savignyplatz. Map p 107.*

★ kids **Marjellchen** CHARLOTTENBURG *GERMAN* Marjellchen is a rare taste of old Berlin with its menu of hearty Prussian dishes. Choose from beetroot soup, home-made aspic with fried potatoes, or flavorsome *Königsberger Klopse* (meatballs in a creamy lemon-caper sauce). Kids and vegetarians are well catered for. *Mommsenstrasse 9.* ☎ *030-883-26-76. Entrees 10.50€–21€. Dinner daily. S-Bahn: Savignyplatz. Map p 107.*

★ Maultaschen Manufaktur

MITTE *GERMAN* Here the emphasis is on the greatest of Swabian dishes, *Maultaschen,* a kind of pasta pocket filled with minced meat, herbs, spinach, and breadcrumbs. All freshly prepared and served either in a broth or browned in butter. *Lützowstrasse 22.* ☎ *017-85-64-76-45. Entrees 8€–11€. MC, V. Dinner Mon–Sat. U-Bahn: Kurfürstenstrasse. Map p 108.*

★ Mey CHARLOTTENBURG TURK-

ISH Step inside this vaulted restaurant for authentic Turkish cuisine. The emphasis is on well-balanced Anatolian flavors, from tender marinated lamb to red lentil soup. *Bleibtreustrasse 47.* ☎ *030-88-68-15-85. Entrees 10€–15€. AE, MC, V. Lunch and dinner daily. S-Bahn: Savignyplatz. Map p 107.*

Dine on authentic Turkish flavours at Mey.

Moon Thai CHARLOTTENBURG *THAI* This reasonably priced Thai den serves up uniformly tasty food—from zingy tom yam soup to tempura and organic tofu. *Kantstrasse 32.* ☎ *030-31-80-97-43. Entrees 8.50€–14.50€. MC, V. Lunch and dinner daily. S-Bahn: Savignyplatz. Map p 107.*

★★ Monsieur Vuong MITTE

VIETNAMESE This hip Vietnamese cafe has carved out an excellent reputation for itself. It's rumored that actor Bruce Willis pops in occasionally to satisfy his cravings for spicy noodles and Saigon beer. Check the blackboard for daily specials. *Alte Schönhauser Strasse 46.* ☎ *030-99-29-69-24. Entrees 6.50€–8€. No credit cards. Lunch and dinner daily. U-Bahn: Weinmeisterstrasse. Map p 108.*

★★ Mr Hai & Friends CHARLOT-

TENBURG *VIETNAMESE* Zesty lime walls, low-level seating, and a potbellied Buddha jazz up this fun Vietnamese restaurant. Watch chefs rustle up tempura and grilled squid in the show kitchen. *Savignyplatz 1.*

Dine at Patio, a barge restaurant on the Spree.

📞 030-37-59-12-00. Entrees 8.50€–14.50€. DC, MC, V. Lunch and dinner daily. S-Bahn: Savignyplatz. Map p 107.

★ **Nu** CHARLOTTENBURG *ASIAN* Nu's pan-Asian menu ranges from Japanese buckwheat noodles with duck and fresh ginger to Vietnamese-style marinated beef with sticky rice. *Schlüterstrasse 55.* 📞 *030-88-70-98-11. Entrees 10€–15€. Lunch and dinner Mon–Sat, dinner Sun. S-Bahn: Savignyplatz. Map p 107.*

★ **Ottenthal** CHARLOTTENBURG *AUSTRIAN* A sleek Kantstrasse restaurant, serving fresh, authentic Austrian cuisine. Specialties include organic boiled beef with horseradish, and venison ragout with bread dumplings. *Kantstrasse 153.* 📞 *030-313-31-62. www.ottenthal.com. Entrees 14€–24€. Dinner daily. U-Bahn: Uhlandstrasse. Map p 107.*

★★★ **Patio** TIERGARTEN *MEDITER-RANEAN* Dine alfresco by the water's edge in summer or by the fireside in winter at this retro-chic barge on the Spree. Tuck into Mediterranean fare such as flaky cod

with polenta and artichokes or wood-oven cooked pizza. *Helgoländer Ufer/Kirchstrasse.* 📞 *030-40-30-17-00. Entrees 11€–23€. MC, V. Oct–Mar dinner daily, lunch Sat–Sun; Apr–Sept lunch and dinner daily. MC, V. S-Bahn: Bellevue. Map p 108.*

★ **Refugium** MITTE *FUSION* This vaulted restaurant by the Franzö-sische Dom serves well-presented, seasonally inspired dishes such as pigeon breast with bolete mush-rooms and suckling pig with a black pudding crust. The chestnut-shaded terrace is a big draw. *Gendarmen-markt 5.* 📞 *030-229-16-61. Entrees 14.50€–32€. AE, MC, V. Lunch and dinner daily. U-Bahn: Französische Strasse. Map p 108.*

★ **Riehmer's** KREUZBERG *AUS-TRIAN* Overlooking Berlin's loveli-est courtyard, this elegant restaurant is tailor-made for a tête-à-tête over Austrian wines and fla-vors such as wild boar goulash and *Tafelspitz* (boiled beef with horse-radish sauce). *Hagelbergerstrasse 9.* 📞 *030-78-89-19-80. Entrees 15€–30€; tasting menu 27.50€. AE, MC,*

V. Dinner Tues–Sun. U-Bahn: Meh-ringdamm. Map p 110.

★★ **Schneeweiss** FRIEDRICHS-HAIN *NOUVELLE GERMAN* With a color scheme as pure as snow and glittering icicle lighting, it's as though Narnia's ice queen designed Schneeweiss. The fare is Alpine: Polish off porcini mushroom risotto and a crisp apple strudel. *Simplon-strasse 16.* ☎ *030-29-04-97-04. www.schneeweiss-berlin.de. Entrees 8€–14.50€. No credit cards. Dinner Mon–Fri, lunch and dinner Sat–Sun. U-Bahn: Frankfurter Tor. Map p 110.*

★ **Schwarzwaldstuben** MITTE *GERMAN* The Black Forest is the inspiration for this cozy, rustic-chic bistro, complete with stag antlers. The flavors, too, are distinctly south-ern German with smoked pork shoulder and *Maultaschen*, a kind of Swabian ravioli, on the menu. *Tucholskystrasse 48.* ☎ *030-28-09-80-84. Entrees 7€–14€. MC, V. Lunch and dinner daily. U-Bahn: Ora-nienburger Tor. Map p 108.*

★★ **Solar** MITTE *FUSION* The best place for a twilight panorama is this glass-walled restaurant-lounge. The pre-dinner ride in an elevator to the 16th floor of an inconspicuous tower block adds to the drama. On the fusion menu are dishes like prawn curry with saffron-mustard-seed rice and tonka-bean crème brulée. *Stresemannstrasse 76.* ☎ *0163-76-52-25-700. www.solar berlin.com. Entrees 17€–35€. MC, V. Dinner daily. S-Bahn: Anhalter Bahn-hof. Map p 108.*

★ **Tafelgold** FRIEDRICHSHAIN *TAPAS* A cozy bohemian-flavored tapas bar offering Spanish and Por-tuguese wines by the glass (from 2.50€) and dates wrapped in ham and baby calamari. It's just steps from Friedrichshain's party mile, Simon-Dach-Strasse. *Niederbarnim-strasse 11.* ☎ *030-74-78-13-64.*

Tapas 2.50€–9€. MC, V. Dinner daily. U-Bahn: Samariterstrasse. Map p 110.

★ **Transit** MITTE *ASIAN* There's always a buzz at this modern Thai-Indonesian outpost, kitted out with communal tables and serving up duck pancakes dripping in plum sauce, catfish red curry, and tangy papaya salad in both small and medium portions. *Rosenthaler Strasse 68.* ☎ *030-24-78-16-45. Entrees 3€–7€. MC, V. Lunch and dinner daily. U-Bahn: Rosenthaler Platz. Map p 108.*

★★★ **Vau** MITTE *MODERN GERMAN* Expect innovative, seasonally inspired flavors at this Michelin-star restaurant—roasted scallops with apple, lentils, and pumpernickel or poached char with beetroot and cocoa. Reservations are essential. *Jägerstrasse 54.* ☎ *030-202-97-30. www.vau-berlin.de. Tasting menus 75€–120€. AE, DC, MC, V. Lunch and dinner Mon–Sat. U-Bahn: Haus-vogteiplatz. Map p 108.*

★★ **Vino e Libri** MITTE *ITALIAN* If the thought of digesting poetry while sipping chianti appeals, seek out this Sardinian restaurant-cum-library. Feast on pasta, gnocchi, or roasted sea bass with stuffed arti-chokes. *Torstrasse 99.* ☎ *030-44-05-84-71. www.vinoelibri.de. Entrees 12€–20€. AE, DC, MC, V. Lunch Mon–Fri, dinner daily. U-Bahn: Rosenthaler Platz. Map p 108.*

★★ **Zur Letzten Instanz** MITTE *GERMAN* Berlin's oldest inn still charms with its wood-paneled inte-rior and witty waiters. Order old-style Berlin favorites such as pickled pork knuckles and blood sausages. *Waisenstrasse 14–16.* ☎ *030-242-55-28. www.zurletzteninstanz.de. Entrees 10€–18€. DC, MC, V. Lunch and dinner Mon–Sat. U-Bahn: Klosterstrasse. Map p 108.* ●

Nightlife Best Bets

Best Twilight Views
★★★ Solar *Stresemannstrasse 76* (p 125)

Best for Tunnel Vision
★ Künstliche BEATmung *Simon-Dach-Strasse 20* (p 124)

Best High-Rise Party
★ Weekend *Alexanderplatz 5* (p 127)

Best Swim & Bop
★★★ Badeschiff *Eichenstrasse 4* (p 126)

Best Beer Garden
★★★ Heinz Minki *Vor dem Schlesischen Tor 3* (p 130)

Best for Watching Sport
★★ Oscar Wilde Pub *Friedrichstrasse 112a* (p 130)

Best Caipirinha on the Beach
★★ Strandgut *Mühlenstrasse 61* (p 126)

Best Moody Blues Bar
★★ Speiches Blueskneipe *Raumerstrasse 39* (p 125)

Open 24 hours a day—Schwarzes Café.

Best Rum Cocktail
★★ Rum Trader *Fasanenstrasse 40* (p 128)

Best Chic Hotel Bar
★ Bebel Bar *Behrenstrasse 37* (p 124)

Best Ballroom Dancing
★★ Clärchens Ballhaus *Auguststrasse 24* (p 126)

Best Techno Club
★★★ Berghain Panorama Bar *Am Wriezener Bahnhof* (p 126)

Best Mixology Magic
★★ Beckett's Kopf Bar *Pappelallee 64* (p 128)

Best Kitsch Gay Bar
★★ Himmelreich *Simon-Dach-Strasse 36* (p 129)

Best Post-Clubbing Breakfast
★★★ Schwarzes Café *Kantstrasse 148* (p 130)

Best Loft Party
★★ Dachkammer *Simon-Dach-Strasse 39* (p 124)

Best Post-Industrial Bar
★ Café Zapata im Kunsthaus Tacheles *Oranienburger Strasse 54* (p 124)

Best See-and-Be-Seen Lounge
★★★ Tausend *Schiffbauerdamm 11* (p 125)

Best GDR-Themed Club
★★ Klub der Republik *Pappelallee 81* (p 127)

Best Club Night
★★ Cookies *Friedrichstrasse 158* (p 126)

Best for Jazz
★★ Victoria Bar *Potsdamer Strasse 102* (p 129)

Best for Couples
★★ Green Door *Winterfeldstrasse 50* (p 128)

Prenzlauer Berg Nightlife

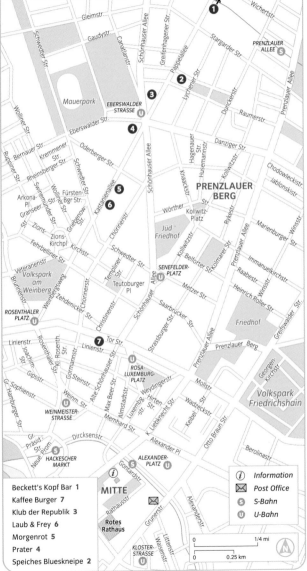

Beckett's Kopf Bar 1
Kaffee Burger 7
Klub der Republik 3
Laub & Frey 6
Morgenrot 5
Prater 4
Speiches Blueskneipe 2

MITTE

Rotes Rathaus

(i) Information
✉ Post Office
Ⓢ S-Bahn
Ⓤ U-Bahn

| 0 | 1/4 mi |
| 0 | 0.25 km |

Previous page: Dachkammer.

Kreuzberg & Friedrichshain

Astro Bar 21
Atlantic 5
Badeschiff 16
Bar Nou 3
Berghain-Panorama Bar 11
Club der Visionäre 14
Dachkammer 20
Freischwimmer 15
Golgatha 1
Haifischbar 2
Heinz Minki 13
Himmelreich 18
Kunstliche BEATmung 17
Paule's Metal Eck 19
Sage 7
Schwuz 4
SO36 9
Strandgut 10
Watergate 12
Weekend 8
Würgeengel 6

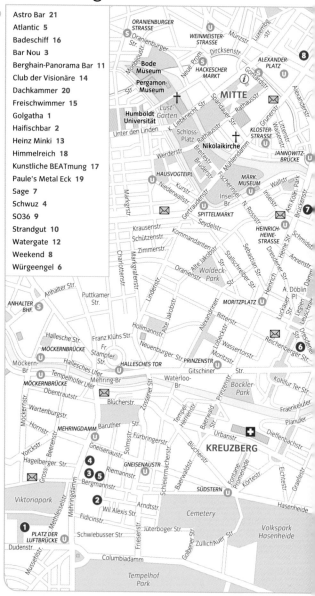

Nightlife

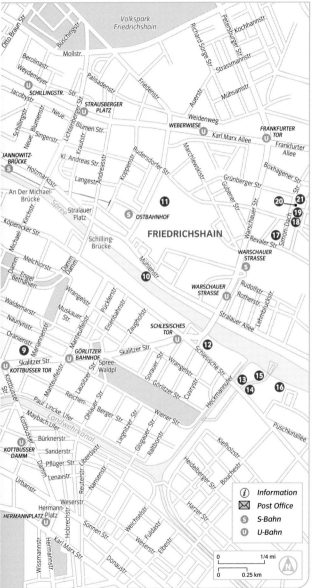

Volkspark
Friedrichshain

Otto Braun Str.
Büschingstr.
Mollstr.
Berolinastr.
Weydemeyer
Jacobystr.
SCHILLINGSTR. Str.
Schillingstr.
Neue Blumenstr.
Neue Singerstr.
Lichtenberger Str.
STRAUSBERGER PLATZ
Blumen Str.
Kraustr.
Andreasstr.
Kl. Andreas Str.
JANNOWITZ-BRÜCKE
Holzmarktstr.
Langestr.
An Der Michael-Brücke
Stralauer Platz
Köpenicker Str.
Michael-Kirchstr.
Melchiorstr.
Damm
Damm
Engel
Bethanien
Wrangelstr.
Waldemarstr.
Muskauer Str.
Naunynstr.
Mariannenstr.
Manteuffelstr.
Oranienstr.
KOTTBUSSER TOR
Skalitzer Str.
GÖRLITZER BAHNHOF
Manteuffelstr.
Skalitzer Str.
Lausitzer Str.
Spree-Waldpl
Reichen
Paul Lincke Ufer
Kottbusser
Maybach Ufer
Kottbusser
KOTTBUSSER DAMM
Bürknerstr.
Sanderstr.
Pflüger Str.
Urbanstr.
Lenavstr.
Reuterstr.
Liberdastr.
Nansenstr.
Weserstr.
HERMANNPLATZ Platz
Hermann-
Hobrechtstr.
Wissmannstr.
Hermannstr.
Karl Marx Str.
Sonnen Str.
Weichselstr.
Weserstr.
Fuldastr.
Elbestr.
Donaustr.

Palisadenstr.
Friedenstr.
Richard Sorge Str.
Petersburger Str.
Kochhannstr.
Strassmannstr.
Auerstr.
Mühsamstr.
Weidenweg
WEBERWIESE
Karl Marx Allee
FRANKFURTER TOR
Frankfurter Allee
Koppenstr.
Rudersdorfer Str.
Marchlewskistr.
Boxhagener Str.
Grünberger Str.
Gubener Str.
Warschauer Str.
FRIEDRICHSHAIN
⑪
Ⓢ OSTBAHNHOF
Schilling-Brücke
Mühlenstr.
⑩
WARSCHAUER STRASSE
Revaler Str.
Simon-Dach Str.
⑳ ㉑
⑲
⑱
⑰
WARSCHAUER STRASSE
Rudolfstr.
Rotherstr.
Lehmbruckstr.
Stralauer Allee
SCHLESISCHES TOR
⑫
Skalitzer Str.
Wrangelstr.
Schlesische Str.
Sorauer Str.
Görlitzer Str.
Cuvrystr.
Heckmannufer
⑬ ⑮
⑭ **⑯**
Ohlauer Str.
Lausitzer Str.
Liegnitzer Str.
Wiener Str.
Glogauer Str.
Ratiborstr.
Püschkinallee
Kiefholzstr.
Heidelberger Str.
Bouchestr.
Harzer Str.

Stralauer Kirchstr.

Spree

Damm

Landwehrkanal

	i	Information
	✉	Post Office
	Ⓢ	S-Bahn
	Ⓤ	U-Bahn

0 ____ 1/4 mi
0 ____ 0.25 km

Mitte & Charlottenburg Nightlife

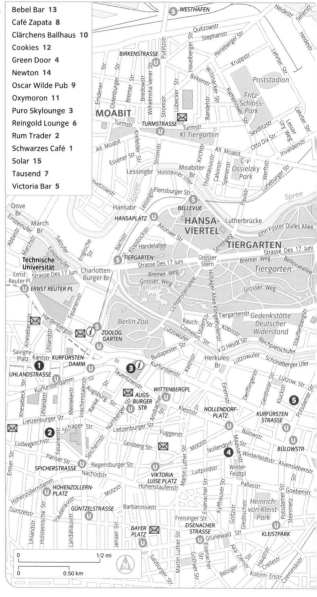

Bebel Bar **13**
Café Zapata **8**
Clärchens Ballhaus **10**
Cookies **12**
Green Door **4**
Newton **14**
Oscar Wilde Pub **9**
Oxymoron **11**
Puro Skylounge **3**
Reingold Lounge **6**
Rum Trader **2**
Schwarzes Café **1**
Solar **15**
Tausend **7**
Victoria Bar **5**

0   1/2 mi
0   0.50 km

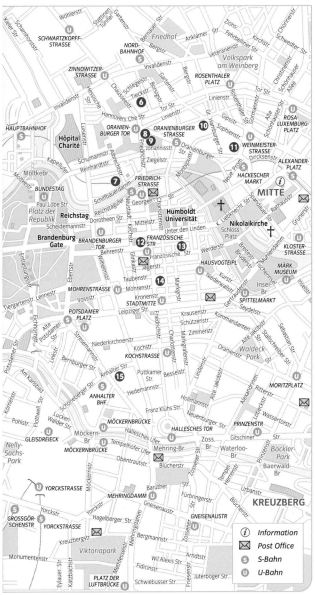

Nightlife A to Z

Bars & Lounge Bars

Astro Bar FRIEDRICHSHAIN Calling all *Hitchhiker* fans! With its black walls, sci-fi kitsch, and threadbare sofas, this cosmic bar is student lounge meets *Star Wars*. Play *Attack from Mars* pinball, ogle the asteroids, and enjoy drinks at prices that are, mercifully, not astronomical. *Simon-Dach-Strasse 40. No phone. U-Bahn: Frankfurter Tor. Map p 120.*

★ **Bebel Bar** MITTE Housed in the former 19th-century Dresdner Bank, the high-ceilinged, subtly lit Bebel Bar is a cocoon of sophistication. Well-to-do Berliners converse over expertly mixed cocktails, mellow music, and views of Bebelplatz. *Behrenstrasse 37.* ☎ *030-460-60-90. U-Bahn: Französische Strasse. Map p 122.*

★★ **Café Zapata** MITTE Industrial-styled decor, tendril-like lights, a fire-breathing dragon and junk art—Zapata is straight off a movie set. Part of Kunsthaus Tacheles (p 122), the dark, moody bar hosts regular DJ nights and gigs (cover 3€–15€). There's a beer garden out back in summer. *Oranienburger Strasse 54.* ☎ *030-281-61-09. www.cafe-zapata. de. U-Bahn: Oranienburger Tor. Map p 122.*

★ **Dachkammer** FRIEDRICHSHAIN The relaxed downstairs bar, with its exposed brickwork, is ideal for quaffing and conversing with young trendies. Upstairs, embrace the 1940s with crimson velvet sofas, gold-striped walls, smooth jazz, and a tiny balcony. *Simon-Dach-Strasse 39.* ☎ *030-296-16-73. U-Bahn: Frankfurter Tor. Map p 120.*

★ **Künstliche BEATmung** FRIED-RICHSHAIN This psychedelic-styled bar centers on a tunnel

The psychedelic interior of retro-style Künstliche BEATmung.

sculpted like a windpipe (the name translates as "artificial breathing"). Drink mojitos as DJs spin house, electro, minimal, and garage to a mixed bunch. *Simon-Dach-Strasse 20.* ☎ *030-70-22-04-72. U-Bahn: Frankfurter Tor. Map p 120.*

★★ **Newton** MITTE A place of quiet sophistication, dressed with leather club chairs, polished oak, and Helmut Newton's risqué shots of nude supermodels. Try a cocktail special like Absolut Newton (vodka, cane sugar, and bitter lemon) at the crescent-shaped bar. *Charlotten-strasse 57.* ☎ *030-202-95-40. U-Bahn: Stadtmitte. Map p 122.*

Paule's Metal Eck FRIEDRICHS-HAIN Goths and vamps head to this down-to-earth pub for solid rock and thrash metal, cheap drinks, and pool. In trendy Friedrichshain,

Paule's breaks the mold with dungeon walls decked out with skulls and dragons. *Krossener Strasse 15.* ☎ *030-291-16-24. U-Bahn: Frankfurter Tor. Map p 120.*

★ **Puro Skylounge** CHARLOTTENBURG While the atmosphere is self-consciously cool, Puro undoubtedly has a captivating panorama of Berlin by night. On the top floor of the Europa Center (take the lift from the side entrance), you'll find a dance floor, champagne bar, and an area for lounging. *Europa Center, Tauentzienstrasse 11.* ☎ *030-26-36-78-75. U-Bahn: Kurfürstendamm. Map p 122.*

★ **Reingold Lounge** MITTE This smart bar for grown-ups evokes the decadent 1930s with gold light panels and caramel leather stools. I like to hobnob over cocktails, as the music moves from retro to jazz and ambient tunes. *Novalisstrasse 11.* ☎ *030-28-38-76-76. U-Bahn: Oranienburger Tor. Map p 122.*

★★★ **Solar** MITTE Arguably the best view of Berlin illuminated is to be had from this sleek, glass-walled lounge on the 17th floor of a nondescript high-rise. Kick back with a drink as the city's landmarks twinkle below. *See p 116. Map p 122.*

★★ **Speiches Blueskneipe** PRENZLAUER BERG Local blues hero Jörg Speiche runs this joint. With grizzled characters, guitars on the walls, and creaking floorboards, it oozes musty charm. Play pool, guzzle beer, and catch one of the regular bands playing blues, rock, or swing. *Raumerstrasse 39.* ☎ *030-444-56-24. U-Bahn: Eberswalder Strasse. Map p 119.*

★★★ **Tausend** MITTE Berlin's most exclusive lounge-bar is located behind an unmarked iron door under a railway bridge. This stylishly urbane affair of curving steel and oversized sofas attracts well-dressed actors, media types, and Berlin's cocktail-sipping glitterati. *Schiffbauerdamm 11.* ☎ *030-41-71-53-96. S-Bahn: Friedrichstrasse. Map p 122.*

★ **Würgeengel** KREUZBERG Scarlet walls and chandeliers shape this smoldering beauty, named after the 1962 movie classic *The Exterminating Angel.* Join arty locals here to

Reingold Lounge catapults you back to the 1930s.

nurse a Pisco sour or a Manhattan and nibble a moreish selection of tapas. *Dresdner Strasse 122.* ☎ *030-615-55-60. U-Bahn: Kottbusser Tor. Map p 120.*

Beach & Canalside Bars

★★★ Badeschiff KREUZBERG

This Spree-side hangout is the place to sway in a hammock, daiquiri in hand, and bop to techno on the beach. The cargo ship pool is perfect for an after-party dip. In winter, it morphs into a floating sauna. *Eichenstrasse 4.* ☎ *030-533-20-30. www.badeschiff.de. Admission 3€. S-Bahn: Ostbahnhof. Map p 120.*

★ Club der Visionäre KREUZBERG

This relaxed and effortlessly cool canal-side shack is packed to the rafters on balmy summer evenings. Young hipsters laze on the deck area, slurp cold beer, and drift away to chill-out music. *Am Flutgraben 1.* ☎ *030-69-51-89-44. U-Bahn: Schlesisches Tor. Map p 120.*

★ Freischwimmer KREUZBERG

It isn't unusual to see locals paddling up to this waterfront bar. When the Berlin Wall stood, there

Chilling on the deck by the water's edge at Club der Visionäre.

was nothing here but allotments; nowadays bright young things spill out onto the deck for drinks with friends. *Vor dem Schlesischen Tor 2a.* ☎ *030-61-07-43-09. U-Bahn: Schlesisches Tor. Map p 120.*

★ Strandgut FRIEDRICHSHAIN

In the summer months this urban beach behind the Berlin Wall offers music, a ship for sunbathing, and zingy caipirinha. A young, hip crowd flocks here to socialize and lounge on white leather sofas under palm trees. *Mühlenstrasse 61.* ☎ *030-70-08-55-66. S-Bahn: Ostbahnhof. Map p 120.*

Clubs

★★★ Berghain-Panorama Bar

FRIEDRICHSHAIN Once a power station, Berghain is now turbo-charged with hardcore revelers who come for the ear-splitting techno, world-class DJs, and a friendly vibe. The club is notorious for its selective and random door policy. *Am Wriezener Bahnhof. www.berghain.de. Cover 8€–12€. S-Bahn: Ostbahnhof. Map p 120.*

★★ Clärchens Ballhaus MITTE

Embrace the glamor of yesteryear in this 19th-century dance hall, complete with dickie-bow-tied waiters and silver tinsel. There's salsa, swing, waltz, and tango every night and you can brush up your footwork at one of the regular dance classes; see the website for details. *Auguststrasse 24.* ☎ *030-282-92-95. www. ballhaus.de. No cover-4€. S-Bahn: Oranienburger Strasse. Map p 122.*

★★ Cookies MITTE

One of Berlin's hottest club nights occurs at Cookies every Tuesday and Thursday. Below the restaurant (p 112) DJs spin techno, house, and hip-hop to a young crowd. Look your best to stand a chance of getting in. *Friedrichstrasse 158.* ☎ *030-442-70-60.*

Chill out by the rooftop pool at Sage.

www.cookies.ch. Cover varies. U-Bahn: Friedrichstrasse. Map p 122.

Kaffee Burger PRENZLAUER BERG A laid-back, arty den where evenings begin with readings, films, or theater, and move swiftly on to DJs pumping out electro, indie, and Balkan beats. The adjacent burger bar is handy for late-night munchies. *Torstrasse 60.* ☎ *030-28-04-64-95. www.kaffeeburger.de. No cover. U-Bahn: Rosa-Luxemburg-Platz. Map p 119.*

★★ **Klub der Republik** PRENZLAUER BERG Up the rickety staircase lies a retro club with a GDR theme. Here you'll find a bunch of good-natured Berliners who come for cheap drinks and DJs cranking out a mix of house, electro, soul, and Sixties grooves. *Pappelallee 81. No phone. No cover. U-Bahn: Eberswalder Strasse. Map p 119.*

Oxymoron MITTE Chandeliers glitter at this glam Hackesche Höfe nightspot. DJs take to the turntables every Friday and Saturday, playing jazz, swing, soul, and funk. *Rosenthaler Strasse 40–41.* ☎ *030-28-39-18-86. www.oxymoron-berlin.de. No cover. S-Bahn: Hackescher Markt. Map p 120.*

★ **Sage** KREUZBERG Dress to the nines to slip past the doormen at this über-cool club where the four dance floors offer up drum and bass, techno, and indie. The orient-inspired decor is swish and the rooftop pool ideal for chilling. *Köpenicker Strasse 76.* ☎ *030-278-98-30. www.sage-club.de. No cover–8€. U-Bahn: Heinrich-Heine-Strasse. Map p 120.*

★ **Watergate** KREUZBERG If you can persuade the surly bouncers to let you in, you'll find pulsating drum and bass anthems, a, glammed-up crowd, and amazing views of the Spree through floor-to-ceiling glass walls in this strikingly lit club. *Falckensteinstrasse 49a.* ☎ *030-61-28-03-96. www.water-gate.de. Cover 8€–12€. U-Bahn: Schlesisches Tor. Map p 120.*

★ **Weekend** KREUZBERG Climb up to the 12th, 15th, and roof-terrace floors of a Soviet-era skyscraper to reach this club. Attracting more tourists than Berliners, it's worth it for the mind-blowing views and top-notch techno. *Alexanderplatz 5.* ☎ *030-24-63-16-76. www.week-end-berlin.de. Cover varies. U-Bahn: Alexanderplatz. Map p 120.*

Karaoke is King

Every Sunday around 3pm, Bonnie Tyler, Michael Jackson, and Britney Spears wannabes descend on the Mauerpark in Prenzlauer Berg for Bearpit Karaoke. Where the Death Strip once stood during the GDR, today Berliners and all-comers gather for a gigantic sing-along with Joe Hatchiban, charismatic Irish entertainer and event founder. Some 2,000 people flock to the small amphitheater, where the music and good vibes just keep flowing. Whether pitch perfect or tone deaf, those who choose to sing (and often dance) drive the crowd wild. From spring to summer, this is one of Berlin's most fun afternoons out. For details, visit www.bearpitkaraoke.com.

Cocktail Bars

★★ **Bar Nou** KREUZBERG Backlit red and gold, this minimalist lounge bar fizzes with fashionable Kreuzbergers. The bar tenders mix a great cocktail—including signatures like spicy Islay Honey (malt whiskey, ginger, lime, and agave syrup). *Bergmannstrasse 104. ☎ 030-74-07-30-50. U-Bahn: Mehringdamm. Map p 120.*

Sip a Shaolin Iced Tea at trendy Bar Nou on Bergmanstrasse.

★★ **Beckett's Kopf Bar** PRENZLAUER BERG There's magic in the mixology at this ever-popular bar. Jazzy tunes create a backdrop for imaginative cocktails like Monkey Gland (gin, grenadine, fresh orange juice, and absinthe). *Pappelallee 64. www.becketts-kopf.de. U-Bahn: Eberswalder Strasse. Map p 119.*

★★ **Green Door** CHARLOTTENBURG Ring the bell on the eponymous green door to be buzzed into this tiny retro cocktail lounge, where Berliners test out "the power of positive drinking." Try the taste-bud-awakening blend of pisco, mint, lemon, cane sugar, and champagne. *Winterfeldstrasse 50. ☎ 030-215-25-15. U-Bahn: Nollendorfplatz. Map p 122.*

★ **Haifischbar** KREUZBERG Sharks guard the door to this Kreuzberg haunt. The jazzy bar serves a winning combination of cocktails—try a ginger martini or a pisco-laced Mariachi—and appetizing Spanish tapas. Happy hour is from 7 to 9pm daily. *Arndtstrasse 25. ☎ 030-691-13-52. U-Bahn: Gneisenaustrasse. Map p 120.*

★★ **Rum Trader** CHARLOTTENBURG Ring the bell to enter this microscopic cocktail bar patronized

Schwarzes Café is open 24-hours.

by a well-heeled Berlin set who are on first-name terms with the bartender. Rum-based cocktails are the specialty here—the Mai Tai is superb. *Fasanenstrasse 40. ☎ 030-881-14-28. U-Bahn: Spichernstrasse. Map p 122.*

★★ **Victoria Bar** MITTE This chi-chi lounge has been designed with a razor-sharp eye for detail, from the walnut paneling to olive leather sofas. Stefan Weber expertly mixes cocktails, so you can sip a Singapore Sling as smooth jazz plays. *Potsdamer Strasse 102. ☎ 030-25-75-99-77. U-Bahn: Kurfürstenstrasse. Map p 122.*

Gay & Lesbian Bars/Clubs

★★ **Himmelreich** FRIEDRICHS-HAIN Golden cherubs and glitter balls, gilded mirrors and mulberry walls—everything about Himmelreich is beautiful. It screams shabby chic with a boho vibe and Motown rhythms. Drinks are 2-for-1 on Wednesdays. *Simon-Dach-Strasse 36. ☎ 030-707-28-306. U-Bahn: Frankfurter Tor. Map p 120.*

★ **Schwuz** KREUZBERG An industrial-style basement club with thrashing sounds and a young (mostly gay) crowd. DJs dominate

the decks with everything from funky R&B beats to Seventies disco and retro hits! *Mehringdamm 61. ☎ 030-629-08-80. Cover 5€–7€. U-Bahn: Mehringdamm. Map p 120.*

★★ **SO36** KREUZBERG This mixed gay-lesbian-straight club presents a varied musical line-up from Asian house to techno, punk, and funk. It also stages regular concerts and wacky themed events. *Oranien-strasse 190. ☎ 030-61-40-13-06. www.so36.de. Cover 10€–24€. U-Bahn: Kottbusser Tor. Map p 122.*

Late-Night Cafes

Atlantic KREUZBERG Unwind with a cold beer on Atlantic's heated terrace, strategically placed for absorbing the action on Bergmannstrasse. Don't miss the quirky flourishes inside, from Betty Boo stamp creations to coffee-bean tables. *Bergmannstrasse 100. ☎ 030-691-92-92. U-Bahn: Mehringdamm. Map p 120.*

Laub & Frey PRENZLAUER BERG Sparkly disco balls and low-level seating set the scene at this cafebar. Come here for inexpensive drinks on the terrace, or shake your stuff as DJs play electro and house to a boho crowd. *Kastanienallee 79.*

Locals chill on the pavement terrace of Heinz Minki.

☎ 030-60-93-05-29. *U-Bahn: Eberswalder Strasse. Map p 119.*

Morgenrot PRENZLAUER BERG Alternative and down-at-heel, this collective cafe embraces folk from all walks of life. Rub shoulders with local artists and sample vegan cocktails, play chess, or catch one of the ad-hoc concerts. It's usually jam-packed. *Kastanienallee 85.* ☎ *030-44-31-78-44. U-Bahn: Eberswalder Strasse. Map p 119.*

★★ Schwarzes Café CHARLOT-TENBURG   This 24-hour cafe is a Kantstrasse institution. The jazzy soundtrack creates a relaxed setting to sip coffee with a pre- and post-clubbing crowd, chat with the chirpy staff, or devour a round-the-clock breakfast. *Kantstrasse 148.* ☎ *030-313-80-38. S-Bahn: Savignyplatz. Map p 122.*

Pubs & Beer Gardens

★ Golgatha KREUZBERG   Kreuzbergers make for Viktoriapark on summer evenings. Golgatha has a laid-back crowd, self-service snacks, and boogying from dusk till dawn. *See p 21. Map p 120.*

★★ Heinz Minki KREUZBERG From summertime parties to Sunday brunch, this shaded garden is a perennial favorite, serving great beer and pizza. Chat with the locals or play table football (soccer) in the 1970s-style living room. *See p 21. Map p 120.*

★★ Oscar Wilde Pub MITTE   An Irish watering hole with big-screen sports. The pub satisfies expat cravings with banter, bacon sandwiches, and Guinness on tap. There's free live music and karaoke or DJ nights at 10pm every Friday and Saturday. *Friedrichstrasse 112a.* ☎ *030-282-81-66. U-Bahn: Oranienburger Tor. Map p 122.*

★★★ Prater PRENZLAUER BERG With a brewing tradition dating back to 1837, this is the granddaddy of Berlin's beer gardens. Sit under the chestnut trees, enjoy Prater pils, and drink in the atmosphere of a vibrant neighborhood. *See p 23. Map p 119.* ●

8

Arts & Entertainment Best Bets

Best Cabaret
★★★ Bar Jeder Vernunft
Schaperstrasse 24 (p 135)

Best Jazz Club
★★★ Quasimodo Kantstrasse 12a
(p 138)

Best Avant-Garde Opera
★★ Komische Oper Behrenstrasse
55–57 (p 136)

Best Orchestral Acoustics
★★★ Berliner Philharmoniker
Herbert-von-Karajan-Strasse 1
(p 136)

Best for Rock & Indie
Concerts
★★ Columbia Halle Columbiadamm
13–21 (p 137)

Best for Drama Classics
★★★ Deutsches Theater
Schumannstrasse 13a (p 138)

Best Opera House
★★★ Staatsoper Unter den Linden
Unter den Linden 7 (p 136)

Best Arthouse Cinema
★ Arsenal Potsdamer Strasse 2
(p 137)

Best for Classical Concerts
★ Konzerthaus Gendarmenmarkt 2
(p 136)

Best for Cutting-Edge Culture
★★★ Kulturbrauerei Schönhauser
Allee 36 (p 137)

Best for Glitzy Vaudeville
★★★ FriedrichstadtPalast Friedrichstrasse 107 (p 135)

Best for Jazz Jam Sessions
★★★ A-Trane Bleibtreustrasse 1
(p 137)

Best Burlesque Show
★★ Kleine Nachtrevue Kurfürstenstrasse 116 (p 135)

Best for Football Fans
★★ Hertha BSC Olympiastadion
(p 138)

Best for Musicals
Theater des Westens Kantstrasse 12
(p 138)

Sally and the Kit Kat Girls, Cabaret, Bar Jeder Vernunft.

Charlottenburg A&E

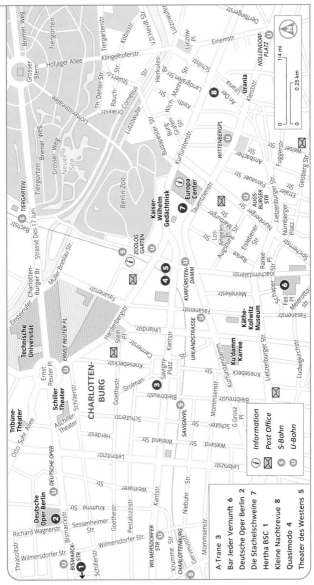

A-Trane 3
Bar Jeder Vernunft 6
Deutsche Oper Berlin 2
Die Stachelschweine 7
Hertha BSC 1
Kleine Nachtrevue 8
Quasimodo 4
Theater des Westens 5

Information
Post Office
S-Bahn
U-Bahn

Previous page: TIPI.

Mitte & Tiergarten **A&E**

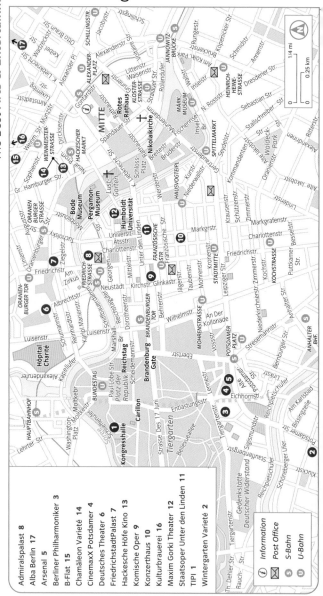

Admiralspalast **8**
Alba Berlin **17**
Arsenal **5**
Berliner Philharmoniker **3**
B-Flat **15**
Chamäleon Varieté **14**
CinemaxX Potsdamer **4**
Deutsches Theater **6**
FriedrichstadtPalast **7**
Hackesche Höfe Kino **13**
Komische Oper **9**
Konzerthaus **10**
Kulturbrauerei **16**
Maxim Gorki Theater **12**
Staatsoper Unter den Linden **11**
TIPI **1**
Wintergarten Varieté **2**

ⓘ	Information
✕	Post Office
Ⓢ	S-Bahn
Ⓤ	U-Bahn

Arts & Entertainment A to Z

Cabaret & Vaudeville

★★★ Bar Jeder Vernunft CHAR-LOTTENBURG Home of the Mirror Tent that twinkled in the movie *Cabaret,* Bar Jeder Vernunft evokes the glamorous Roaring Twenties. The first-rate comedy and chanson performances whisk you back to Sally Bowles at the Kit Kat Club. *Schaperstrasse 24.* ☎ *030-883-15-82. www.bar-jeder-vernunft.de. Tickets 22€–60€. U-Bahn: Spichernstrasse. Map p 133.*

Chamäleon Varieté MITTE For circus-style slapstick, head to this informal theater in the Hackesche Höfe. From clowns to jugglers and aerialists, the eclectic variety acts keep the young crowd in fits of giggles. *Hackesche Höfe.* ☎ *030-400-05-90. www.chamaeleon-variete.de. Tickets 34€–45€. S-Bahn: Hackescher Markt. Map p 134.*

★ Die Stachelschweine CHAR-LOTTENBURG A staple in Berlin's entertainment diet, "the porcupines" theater stages excellent literary cabaret (in German) where performances prickle with sharp political satire. *Europa Center.* ☎ *030-261-47-95. www.stachelschweine-berlin.de. Tickets 13€–28€. U-Bahn: Zoologischer Garten. Map p 133.*

★★★ FriedrichstadtPalast MITTE Europe's largest revue theater presents an exuberant feast of sequin-studded costumes, vaudeville performances, and leggy showgirls. *Friedrichstrasse 107.* ☎ *030-23-26-23-26. www.friedrichstadtpalast.de. Tickets 17€–105€. S-Bahn: Friedrichstrasse. Map p 134.*

★★ Kleine Nachtrevue CHAR-LOTTENBURG This small theater catapults you back to 1920s Berlin. It's feted for burlesque performances that are risqué but not lewd, creating a successful blend of erotica and nostalgia with satirical undertones. *Kurfürstenstrasse 116.*

Catch a glittering revue performance at FriedrichstadtPalast.

☎ 030-218-89-50. www.kleine-nachtrevue.de. Tickets 20€–30€. U-Bahn: Wittenbergplatz. Map p 133.

TIPI TIERGARTEN This meringue-like marquee, between Haus der Kulturen der Welt and the Bundes-kanzleramt, stages chanson, cabaret, variety theater, dance, and musical comedy. *Grosse Querallee.* ☎ 030-39-06-65-50. www.tipi-das-zelt.de. Tickets 25€–55€. S-Bahn: Unter den Linden. Map p 134.

★★ Wintergarten Varieté

MITTE Berlin's most celebrated variety theater welcomes a fanfare of trapeze artists, contortionists, and clowns, all beneath a star-studded ceiling. *Potsdamer Strasse 96.* ☎ 030-58-84-33. www.wintergarten-variete.de. Tickets 19.50€–54.50€. U-Bahn: Kurfürstenstrasse. Map p 134.

Classical, Opera & Ballet
★★★ Berliner Philharmoniker

MITTE Hans Scharoun's asymmetrical concert hall is home to the high-profile Berlin Philharmonic Orchestra. Performances include contemporary

Carmen at Staatsoper Unter den Linden.

and chamber music. *Herbert-von-Karajan-Strasse 1.* ☎ 030-25-48-89-99. www.berliner-philharmoniker.de. Tickets 7€–140€. S-Bahn: Potsdamer Platz. Map p 134.

★★ Deutsche Oper Berlin

CHARLOTTENBURG There are doubtless more aesthetically attractive venues, but it's what happens here that counts. Alongside productions such as Mozart's *Magic Flute*, the venue stages regular classical concerts, recitals, and ballet. *Bismarckstrasse 35.* ☎ 030-34-38-43-43. www.deutscheoperberlin.de. Tickets 5€–120€. U-Bahn: Deutsche Oper. Map p 133.

★★ Komische Oper MITTE

The opulent hall of this high-caliber opera house resembles a giant Fabergé egg. Avant-garde opera, musical theater, and ballet are performed in German. *Behrenstrasse 55–57.* ☎ 030-47-99-74-00. www.komische-oper-berlin.de. Tickets 10€–93€. U-Bahn: Französische Strasse. Map p 134.

★ Konzerthaus MITTE Mozart

once took the stage by storm and Beethoven's Symphony No. 9 premiered at this grand concert hall, still as popular today with classical music lovers. Home to the Deutsches Sinfonie-Orchester and innovative conductor Lothar Zagrosek. *Gendarmenmarkt 2.* ☎ 030-203-09-21-01. www.konzerthaus.de. Tickets 13€–99€. U-Bahn: Französische Strasse: Map p 134.

★★★ Staatsoper Unter den

Linden MITTE Strauss was once chief conductor at Berlin's oldest opera house. Today, the swish venue provides a stage for opera, chamber concerts, recitals, and ballet of remarkable quality. *Unter den Linden 7; box office Bismarckstrasse 110.* ☎ 030-20-35-45-55. www.staatsoper-berlin.org. Tickets 14€–160€. U-Bahn: Französische Strasse. Map p 134.

Tickets & Listings

Pick up a copy of the bi-weekly magazine Tip (www.tip-berlin.de; in German), 3.20€, for up-to-date concert, theater, and events listings. Most venues let you pre-book tickets online or by phone. Ticket agencies are another option, but be prepared to pay a 10–15% booking fee. The online booking service **Hekticket** (☎ 030-230-99-30; www.hekticket.de) accepts all major credit cards and posts tickets worldwide; half-price tickets are often available for same-day performances from **ticket booths** at Hardenbergstrasse 29 (opposite Zoologischer Garten station) and Karl-Liebknecht-Strasse 13 (Alexanderplatz S-Bahn station).

Film

★ **Arsenal** MITTE   This excellent cinema on Potsdamer Platz screens art-house films: from silent movies to French classics and retrospectives. Most are shown in their original language. *Potsdamer Strasse 2.* ☎ *030-26-95-51-00. www.arsenal-berlin.de. Tickets 6.50€. S-Bahn: Potsdamer Platz. Map p 134.*

CinemaxX Potsdamer MITTE Hollywood blockbusters and mainstream releases attract cinemagoers to this 19-screen multiplex on Potsdamer Platz. Most are in German only. *Potsdamer Strasse 5.* ☎ *01805-24-63-62-99. www.cinemaxx.de. Tickets 5€–7.50€. S-Bahn: Potsdamer Platz. Map p 134.*

Hackesche Höfe Kino MITTE This theater set in the Art Nouveau courtyards of Hackesche Höfe reels in movie buffs with a line-up of artistic and experimental film. *Hackesche Höfe.* ☎ *030-283-46-03. www.hackesche-hoefe.org. Tickets 6.50€–8€. S-Bahn: Hackescher Markt. Map p 134.*

Live Music

★★★ **A-Trane** CHARLOTTENBURG This friendly jazz club has seen the likes of Diana Krall, Alice Coltrane, and Herbie Hancock perform in the past. Don't miss Saturday's free late-night jam sessions. *Bleibtreustrasse 1.* ☎ *030-313-25-50. www.a-trane.de. Cover 8€–30€. S-Bahn: Savignyplatz. Map p 133.*

B-Flat MITTE   The emphasis here is on modern jazz and acoustic music, stretching from world rhythms to Latin beats, bebop to big bands. On Wednesdays there's free entry to Robin Draganic's jam sessions. *Rosenthaler Strasse 13.* ☎ *030-283-31-23. www.b-flat-berlin.de. Cover free–12€. U-Bahn: Rosenthaler Platz. Map p 134.*

★★ **Columbia Halle** TEMPELHOF Columbia Halle is Berlin's top stage for rock, pop, and indie concerts. Recent headliners include Bonaparte and The Sisters of Mercy. *Columbiadamm 13–21.* ☎ *030-698-09-80. www.columbiahalle.de. Tickets 20€–60€. U-Bahn: Platz der Luftbrücke.*

★★★ **Kulturbrauerei** PRENZLAUER BERG   This gigantic cultural complex occupies the former Schultheiss Brewery. The program is diverse, comprising opera, dance, theater, festivals, concerts, and film screenings. You'll also find clubs, bars, and restaurants on site. *Schönhauser Allee 36.* ☎ *030-44-31-51-51.*

www.kulturbrauerei.de. Ticket prices vary. U-Bahn: Eberswalder Strasse. Map p 134.

★★★ Quasimodo CHARLOTTEN-BURG

This basement is jam-packed most nights with a lineup alternating big names with local talent. The venue occasionally embraces blues, Latin, or rock. Don't miss Wednesday night's live jam (tickets 5€). *Kantstrasse 12a.* ☎ *030-312-80-86. www.quasimodo.de. Cover 5€–24€. U-Bahn: Zoologischer Garten. Map p 133.*

Spectator Sports

Alba Berlin PRENZLAUER BERG Basketball fans pile into Max-Schmeling-Halle arena to catch one of Alba Berlin's home matches (Sept–May). The team has a string of Bundesliga titles and German Cups to its name. *Am Falkplatz.* ☎ *030-30-09-05-55. www.albaberlin.de. Tickets 10€–55€. U-Bahn: Schönhauser Allee. Map p 134.*

★★ Hertha BSC CHARLOTTEN-BURG

Berlin's Olympic Stadium, which hosted the final of the 2006 football (soccer) World Cup, is the stomping ground of German league club Hertha BSC. Match tickets are usually available on the day. *Olympiastadion.* ☎ *01805-18-92-00. www.herthabsc.de. Tickets 9.50€–35.50€. S-Bahn: Olympiastadion. Map p 133.*

Theater

★ Admiralspalast MITTE

This Art Deco theater was a major stomping ground in the 1920s, when it was a cabaret, spa, and brothel. Alongside theater productions, you'll find thermal baths, a cafe, and a nightclub. *Friedrichstrasse 101–102.* ☎ *030-47-99-74-99. www.admiralspalast.de. Tickets 13€–31€. S-Bahn: Friedrichstrasse. Map p 134.*

★★★ Deutsches Theater MITTE

The varied repertoire at this elegant 19th-century theater ranges from classics such as Shakespeare's *A Midsummer Night's Dream* (in German) to Friedrich Dürrenmatt's *Die Physiker*. *Schumannstrasse 13a.* ☎ *030-28-44-12-25. www.deutschestheater.de. Tickets 7€–43€. U-Bahn: Oranienburger Tor. Map p 134.*

★ Maxim Gorki Theater MITTE

Expect a scintillating program featuring the likes of Goethe's *The Sorrows of Young Werther* or Molière's comic drama *Amphitryon*. Young German playwrights also feature prominently. *Am Festungsgraben 2.* ☎ *030-20-22-11-15. www.gorki.de. Tickets 10€–32€. S-Bahn: Friedrichstrasse. Map p 134.*

Theater des Westens CHARLOTTENBURG

Josephine Baker and Marlene Dietrich both performed at this glorious Art Nouveau theater. Nowadays it stages musicals in German, such as *The Three Musketeers* and *Tanz der Vampire*. *Kantstrasse 12.* ☎ *030-31-90-30. Ticket prices vary. U-Bahn: Zoologischer Garten. Map p 133.* ●

Stucco sculptures grace the facade of Theater des Westens.

9

The Best **Lodging**

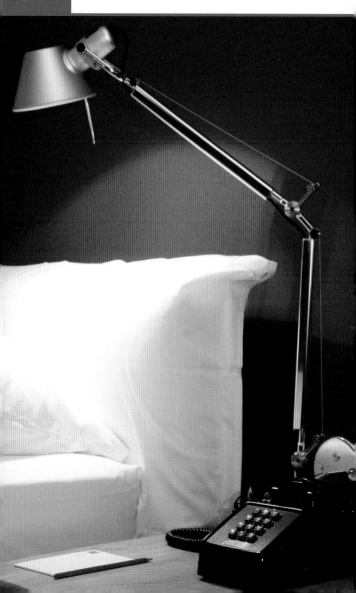

Lodging Best Bets

Best for **Wild Bedrooms**
★★ Arte Luise Kunsthotel *Luisenstrasse 19 (p 145)*

Best **1920s Flashback**
★★★ Askanischer Hof
Kurfürstendamm 53 (p 145)

Best **Hotel on Water**
★★ Eastern Comfort *Mühlenstrasse 73–77 (p 146)*

Best **Eco-Conscious Hotel**
★★★ Circus Hotel *Rosenthaler Strasse 1 (p 146)*

Best **Design Hotel**
★★★ Casa Camper *Weinmeisterstrasse 1 (p 146)*

Best for **Art Nouveau Style**
★★★ Hotel Art Nouveau *Leibnizstrasse 59 (p 147)*

Best **On a Budget**
★★★ EastSeven Hostel *Schwedter Strasse 7 (p 146)*

The shapely Art Nouveau entrance to Askanischer Hof on Kurfürstendamm.

Best for a **Romantic Weekend**
★★ Honigmond Garden Hotel
Invalidenstrasse 122 (p 146)

Best **Colombian Charm**
★ Hotel Bogota *Schlüterstrasse 45 (p 147)*

Best for **Old-World Opulence**
★★★ Hotel Adlon Kempinski *Unter den Linden 77 (p 147)*

Best **Courtyard**
★★ Hotel Riehmers Hofgarten
Yorckstrasse 83 (p 148)

Best **Boutique Hotels**
★★ Bleibtreu Hotel *Bleibtreustrasse 31 (p 145)*; and ★★ Hotel Otto *Knesebeckstrasse 10 (p 147)*

Best **Celebrity Magnet**
★ Hotel Q! *Knesebeckstrasse 67 (p 147)*

Best **NY Loft-Style Apartments**
★ Adele Hotel *Greifswalder Strasse 227 (p 145)*

Best **Spa**
★★ Ku'Damm 101 *Kurfürstendamm 101 (p 148)*

Best **Asian-Inspired Design**
★★★ Mandala Hotel *Potsdamer Strasse 3 (p 149)*

Best **Rooftop Terrace**
★ Upstalsboom Hotel *Gubener Strasse 42 (p 150)*

Best for **Avant-Garde Luxury**
★★ Westin Grand *Friedrichstrasse 158–164 (p 150)*

Best **Villa Hideaway**
★★ Pension Rotdorn *Heerstrasse 36 (p 150)*

Best **Business Hotel**
★ Courtyard Berlin City Center
Axel-Springer-Strasse 55 (p 146)

Best for **Families**
★ Agon Frankfurter Allee *Scharnweberstrasse 21–22 (p 145)*

Charlottenburg & Tiergarten
Lodging

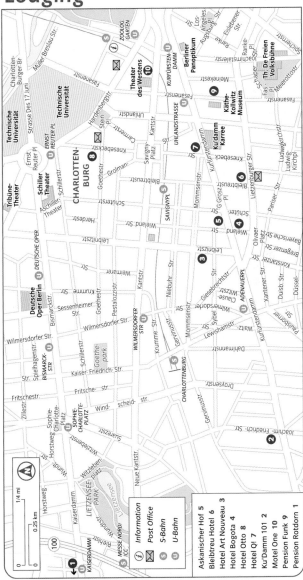

Askanischer Hof 5
Bleibtreu Hotel 6
Hotel Art Nouveau 3
Hotel Bogota 4
Hotel Otto 8
Hotel QI 7
Ku'Damm 101 2
Motel One 10
Pension Funk 9
Pension Rotdorn 1

Previous page: Hotel Casa Camper.

Mitte & Prenzlauer Berg **Lodging**

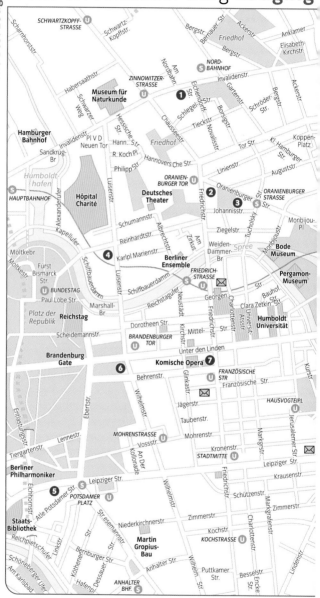

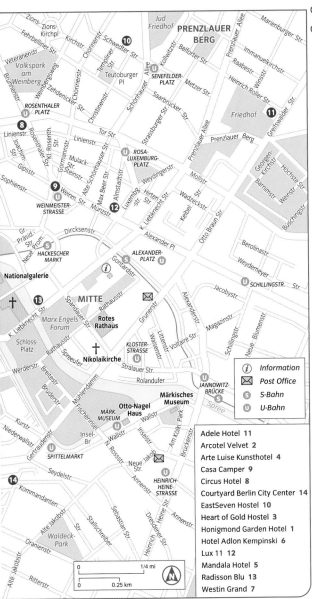

Adele Hotel **11**	
Arcotel Velvet **2**	
Arte Luise Kunsthotel **4**	
Casa Camper **9**	
Circus Hotel **8**	
Courtyard Berlin City Center **14**	
EastSeven Hostel **10**	
Heart of Gold Hostel **3**	
Honigmond Garden Hotel **1**	
Hotel Adlon Kempinski **6**	
Lux 11 **12**	
Mandala Hotel **5**	
Radisson Blu **13**	
Westin Grand **7**	

Legend

i Information

✉ Post Office

S S-Bahn

U U-Bahn

Kreuzberg & Friedrichshain
Lodging

Agon Frankfurter Allee **5**
Eastern Comfort **2**
Hotel Riehmers Hofgarten **1**
Hotel 26 **4**
Upstalsboom Hotel **3**

Post Office
S-Bahn
U-Bahn

Lodging A to Z

Adele Hotel PRENZLAUER BERG
The spacious rooms here recall New York loft apartments with wood floors, clean hues, and modern touches from velvet throws to Bauhaus-inspired furniture. *Greifswalder Strasse 227. ☎ 030-44-32-43-10. www.adele-hotel.de. 14 units. Doubles 109-149€ w/breakfast. AE, MC, V. S-Bahn: Greifswalder Strasse. Map p 142.*

★ kids Agon Frankfurter Allee
FRIEDRICHSHAIN   This townhouse tucked down a cobbled street has been lovingly restored. Mediterranean colors give the spacious rooms warmth, and staff will happily supply an extra children's bed if you ask. *Scharnweberstrasse 21–22. ☎ 030-297-77-70. www.agon-frankfurter-allee.de. 73 units. Doubles 55€–129€. AE, DC, MC, V. U-Bahn: Samariterstrasse. Map p 144.*

★★ Arcotel Velvet MITTE   Huge windows allow plenty of daylight into the rooms combining dark wood, wine-red fabrics, and Pop Art elements. Flat-screen TVs and DVD players add a high-tech touch. *Oranienburger Strasse 52. ☎ 030-278-75-30. www.arcotel.at. 85 units. Doubles 85€–189€. AE, MC, V. S-Bahn: Oranienburger Strasse. Map p 142.*

★★ Arte Luise Kunsthotel
MITTE   There are few hotels where you can sleep surrounded by gold spray-painted bananas or in a cabaret-inspired bedroom. To avoid noise from the railway request a courtyard-facing room. *Luisenstrasse 19. ☎ 030-28-44-80. www.luise-berlin.com. 50 units. Doubles 99€–210€. MC, V. S-Bahn: Friedrichstrasse. Map p 142.*

★★★ kids Askanischer Hof
CHARLOTTENBURG   This bijou hotel propels you back to the early 20th century. The high-ceilinged rooms are adorned with pot plants and hat stands, while black-and-white photos of 1920s starlets festoon the dining room. *Kurfürstendamm 53. ☎ 030-881-80-33. www.askanischer-hof.de. 16 units. Doubles 120€–180€ w/breakfast. AE, MC, V. S-Bahn: Savignyplatz. Map p 141.*

★★ Bleibtreu Hotel CHARLOTTENBURG   Bleibtreu is a boutique hotel, set inside a 19th-century patrician house, with spacious, light rooms. Alongside Wi-Fi, you find an apple beside your bed and a free minibar. *Bleibtreustrasse 31. ☎ 030-88-47-40. www.bleibtreu.com. 60 units. Doubles 118€–198€. AE, DC, MC, V. S-Bahn: Savignyplatz. Map p 141.*

Apples become works of art at Bleibtreu Hotel.

★★★ Casa Camper MITTE
Camper's minimalist, boutique design hotel bears the imprint of Spanish designer Fernando Amat and architect Jordi Tio. The major draw for foodies is über-stylish Dos Palillos, serving delectable Asian tapas. *Weinmeisterstrasse 1.* ☎ *030-20-00-34-10. www.casacamper.com. 51 units. Doubles 205€–305€ w/ breakfast. AE, DC, MC, V. U-Bahn: Weinmeisterstrasse. Map p 142.*

★★★ Circus Hotel MITTE
It's the personal touches that make the difference at this modestly priced, eco-conscious boutique hotel. The individually designed rooms have rain showers, minimalist furnishings, and Wi-Fi. *Rosenthaler Strasse 1.* ☎ *030-20-00-39-39. www.circus-berlin.de. 65 units. Doubles 80€–110€. AE, MC, V. U-Bahn: Rosenthaler Platz. Map p 142.*

★ Courtyard Berlin City Center
MITTE   Business travelers choose this value-for-money Marriott hotel for its central location. Rooms have high-speed Internet access and laptop-size safes. Facilities include a

Four-poster romance at Honigmond Garden Hotel.

sauna and a gym. *Axel-Springer-Strasse 55.* ☎ *030-800-92-80. www.marriott.com. 276 units. Doubles 99€–250€. AE, DC, MC, V. U-Bahn: Spittelmarkt. Map p 142.*

★★ Eastern Comfort FRIEDRICH-SHAIN
For sheer novelty value, check into this riverboat moored on the Spree. Opt for a cozy double cabin with portholes, or bed down in the bunkroom. You'll find fellow drifters sipping cold beer under the stars on the upper deck. Free Wi-Fi. *Mühlenstrasse 73–77.* ☎ *030-66-76-38-06. www.eastern-comfort.com. 25 units. Doubles 58€–78€. MC, V. S-Bahn: Ostbahnhof. Map p 144.*

★★★ kids EastSeven Hostel
PRENZLAUER BERG   Upping the ante in the budget stakes is this retro-style hostel, where cheery staff make backpackers feel at home with perks such as free Wi-Fi and walking tours. *Schwedter Strasse 7.* ☎ *030-93-62-22-40. www.eastseven.de. Beds 14€–38€. MC, V. U-Bahn: Senefelder Platz. Map p 142.*

Heart of Gold Hostel MITTE
Rooms here are spacey, spotless, and a bargain, given the central location. Plus the hostel offers amenities to make budget travelers' hearts sing: free Wi-Fi, cheap drinks, and no curfew. *Johannisstrasse 11.* ☎ *030-29-00-33-00. www.heartof gold-hostel.de. 46 units. Beds 10€–32€. AE, MC, V. U-Bahn: Friedrich-strasse. Map p 142.*

★★ Honigmond Garden Hotel
MITTE   Romantics will fall in love with the garden's creeping vines, palms, and croaking frogs. This 19th-century hotel's high-ceilinged rooms are also a joy, decorated with hardwood floors, stucco, and antiques. *Invalidenstrasse 122.* ☎ *030-28-44-55-77. www.honigmond-berlin.de. 44 units. Doubles 125€–230€ w/ breakfast. MC, V. S-Bahn: Berlin-Nordbahnhof. Map p 142.*

A suite at Hotel Adlon Kempinski with views to the Brandenburg Gate.

★★★ Hotel Adlon Kempinski

MITTE   Over the years, this palatial hotel has rolled out the red carpet for celebrities including Greta Garbo and Charlie Chaplin. Bedrooms with marble bathrooms present old-school luxury—all at a steep price, mind. *Unter den Linden 77.* ☎ *030-22-61-0. www.hotel-adlon.de. 382 units. Doubles 190€–420€. AE, DC, MC, V. S-Bahn: Unter den Linden. Map p 142.*

★★★ kids Hotel Art Nouveau

CHARLOTTENBURG   An old elevator creaks you up to high-ceilinged rooms with huge windows at this Art Nouveau retreat. Each are styled with individual themes, from monochrome Japanese to sunny yellow. *Leibnizstrasse 59.* ☎ *030-327-74-40. www.hotelartnouveau.de. 20 units. Doubles 116€–186€ w/breakfast. AE, MC, V. S-Bahn: Savignyplatz. Map p 141.*

★ kids Hotel Bogota CHARLOT-

TENBURG   Stay at this hotel for a taste of old-world Colombia in Berlin. Although quite dark, the high-ceilinged rooms are cozy and sensibly priced. *Schlüterstrasse 45.* ☎ *030-881-50-01. www.bogota.de. 130 units. Doubles 64€–150€ w/ breakfast. AE, MC, V. S-Bahn: Savignyplatz. Map p 141.*

★★ kids Hotel Otto CHARLOT-

TENBURG   Don't be fooled by the nondescript facade of this boutique hotel, tucked down a quiet street. Inside you'll be pleasantly surprised by the warm welcome and tasteful rooms—some with walk-in closets. *Knesebeckstrasse 10.* ☎ *030-54-71-00-80. www. hotelotto.com. 46 units. Doubles 14€–38€. MC, V. U-Bahn: Ernst-Reuter Platz. Map p 141.*

★ Hotel Q! CHARLOTTENBURG

Self-consciously hip and flaunting a string of design awards, Q! is a magnet for fashionistas and movie stars such as Brad Pitt. The style isn't elegant; it's vampy with wavy walls, scarlet accents, and low lighting. *Knesebeckstrasse 67.* ☎ *030-810-06-60. www.loock-hotels.com. 77*

The concertina-style columns in the lobby at Ku'Damm 101.

units. Doubles 120€–235€ w/breakfast. AE, DC, MC, V. U-Bahn: Uhlandstrasse. Map p 141.

★★ kids **Hotel Riehmers Hofgarten** KREUZBERG Situated in an Art Nouveau courtyard, this boutique hotel is a real find. The rooms are charming with high ceilings,

stucco, and creaking floors. Saunter downstairs for drinks beside the grand piano or dinner in the excellent French-German restaurant. *Yorckstrasse 83.* ☎ *030-78-09-88-00. www.riehmers-hofgarten.de. 22 units. Doubles 138€–155€ w/breakfast. AE, MC, V. U-Bahn: Mehringdamm. Map p 144.*

★ **Hotel 26** FRIEDRICHSHAIN Stefan Lorenzen worked his magic to revamp a factory into this modern hotel, within staggering distance of Friedrichshain's bars. Rooms are fairly basic and clean, all with cable TV. *Grünberger Strasse 26.* ☎ *030-29-77-78-0. www.hotel26-berlin.de. 22 units. Doubles 79€–99€. AE, MC, V. U-Bahn: Frankfurter Tor. Map p 144.*

★★ **Ku'Damm 101** CHARLOTTENBURG Rooms are slick, decorated in muted tones with bold furniture by leading German designers; 17 are equipped for the visually impaired. You can end your day relaxing in the spa. *Kurfürstendamm 101.* ☎ *030-520-05-50. www.kudamm101.com. 170 units. Doubles 119€–250€. AE, DC, MC, V. U-Bahn: Adenauerplatz. Map p 141.*

Moneysaving Tips

Advance reservations are essential during Berlin's busiest periods: June to September and Christmas/Easter holidays. Outside of these times, you can pick up great deals, particularly if you check in midweek and are flexible about location. In winter (Nov through Feb), crowds are thinner and many hotels drop rates by around 20%. **Berlin Tourist Information** (p 172) offers a free accommodation booking service and best-price guarantee. Most visitors want to stay close to the shops and sights in Mitte and Charlottenburg, so expect more for your euro in edgier districts such as Kreuzberg, Prenzlauer Berg, and Friedrichshain, offering a younger vibe and pulsating nightlife. For discount hotels and last-minute deals, try **Last Minute** (www.lastminute.com), **Hotel.com** (www.hotels.com), and **Late Rooms** (www.laterooms.com).

★ **Lux 11** MITTE   This design hotel has seven floors given over to virginal white and Zen-inspired apartments, boasting fully equipped kitchens and DVD players. Downstairs, you'll find an Italian restaurant, boutique, hair salon, and spa. *Rosa-Luxemburg-Strasse 9–13.* ☎ *030-936-28-00. www.lux-eleven.de. 72 units. Doubles 135€–205€. AE, DC, MC, V. U-Bahn: Alexanderplatz. Map p 142.*

★★★ **Mandala Hotel** MITTE Unpretentiously elegant, the Mandala fuses creature comforts with avant-garde design. After a long day, the sophisticated Qiu cocktail lounge, 11th-floor spa with far-reaching views over Berlin, and Michael Kemp's Facil restaurant await. *Potsdamer Strasse 3.* ☎ *030-590-05-00-00. www.themandala.de. 157 units. Studios and suites 270€–5,800€. AE, DC, MC, V. S-Bahn: Potsdamer Platz. Map p 142.*

★ **Motel One** CHARLOTTENBURG If you sleep like a log despite train noise, this is a good-value and well-located choice. Rooms have flat-screen TVs and granite bathrooms, and the funky lobby bar serves up snacks and free Wi-Fi. *Kantstrasse 7.* ☎ *030-31-51-73-60. www.motel-one. de. 249 units. Doubles 74€–94€. AE, DC, MC, V. U-Bahn: Zoologischer Garten. Map p 141.*

★ **Pension Funk** CHARLOTTEN-BURG   What this charming guesthouse lacks in frills, it makes up for with a top location off Ku'damm. The former home of silent-movie star Asta Nielsen is a flashback to the belle époque. Rooms are old-fashioned yet comfortable, replete with period features and antique furnishings. There's free Wi-Fi. *Fasanenstrasse 69.* ☎ *030-882-71-93. www. hotel-pensionfunk.de. 14 units. Doubles 52€–129€ w/breakfast. MC, V. U-Bahn: Uhlandstrasse. Map p 141.*

The lounge bar at über-cool Hotel Q!

The avant-garde lobby at Berlin's smart Mandala Hotel.

★★ **Pension Rotdorn** CHARLOTTENBURG   Set among tranquil gardens, this 1920s villa is a stone's throw from the Olympic Stadium. The light rooms with velvet furnishings and brass mirrors ooze old-world charm. *Heerstrasse 36.* ☎ *030-30-09-92-92. www.pension-rotdorn.de. 18 units. Doubles 50€– 90€ w/breakfast. No credit cards. S-Bahn: Heerstrasse. Map p 141.*

★★ **Radisson Blu** MITTE   Located on the banks of the River Spree, and housing the world's largest cylindrical aquarium, this hotel's minimalist rooms feature the luxurious trappings that come with their price tag. Unwind in the spa or enjoy alfresco dining. *Karl-Liebknecht-Strasse 3.* ☎ *030-23-82-80. www.radissonblu. com/hotel-berlin. 427 units. Doubles 155€–380€. AE, DC, MC, V. U-Bahn: Alexanderplatz. Map p 142.*

★ **Upstalsboom Hotel** FRIEDRICHSHAIN   Despite the corporate aura, this hotel is a comfortable base with modern rooms in soothing color schemes. Upstairs there's a sauna and lounge on the rooftop terrace. *Gubener Strasse 42.* ☎ *030-29-37-50. www.upstalsboom.de. 170 units. Doubles 99€–254€ w/breakfast. AE, DC, MC, V. S-Bahn: Warschauer Strasse. Map p 144.*

★★ **Westin Grand** MITTE   A grand staircase sweeps up to contemporary rooms with welcome extras such as flat-screen TVs, fluffy bathrobes, and garden or city views. Downtime can be spent in the spa, in the panoramic bar, or over dinner in the restaurant. *Friedrichstrasse 158– 164.* ☎ *030-202-70. www.westin grandberlin.com. 400 units. Doubles 199€–510€. AE, DC, MC, V. U-Bahn: Französische Strasse. Map p 142.* ●

Schloss Charlottenburg & Around

1 Schloss Charlottenburg
2 Schlossgarten
3 Museum Berggruen
4 Bröhan Museum
5 Opera Italiana
6 Sammlung Scharf-Gerstenberg
7 Schlossstrasse
8 Schustrehrus Park
9 Villa Oppenheim

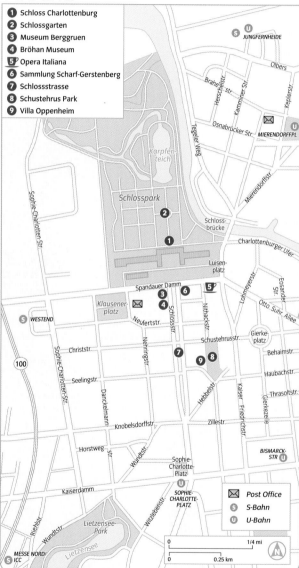

✉		Post Office
Ⓢ		S-Bahn
Ⓤ		U-Bahn

0		1/4 mi
0	0.25 km	

Previous page: Altes Rathaus, Potsdam.

Berlin's petit Versailles, the opulent baroque summer palace of Schloss Charlottenburg, merits at least half a day of your time. Relive the splendor of the Hohenzollern dynasty in gilded state apartments and French gardens strewn with romantic follies. In the afternoon, explore genteel Charlottenburg, where galleries showcase Picasso, Art Nouveau, and Surrealist works. START: **S-Bahn to Westend.**

❶ ★★★ Schloss Charlottenburg. King Friedrich I of Prussia gave this not-so-humble abode to his sweetheart, Sophie Charlotte, as a token of his affection in 1699. The summer palace is the jewel in Berlin's Hohenzollern crown and a feast of Italian baroque. The facade alone is breathtaking, partly modeled on Versailles and adorned with Attica-style sculptures. Note the bronze statue of the king mounted on a horse—a great vantage point if you're feeling snap-happy. The staterooms are overwhelming, so I recommend you concentrate on the **Altes Schloss** (Old Grossen Kurfürsten Palace). You can take in the Great Oak Gallery, an exquisitely carved, oak-paneled banquet hall completed in 1713, the crimson and gold **Red Damask Chamber,** and the king's all-gold Bedchamber. The highlight is the Porcelain Room,

Tree-fringed Schlossstrasse boulevard sweeps up to Schloss Charlottenburg.

brimming with 2,700 pieces of Chinese and Japanese porcelain, from cups to trinkets and vases. ⏱ *1 hr. Spandauer Damm 10–22.* ☎ *030-32-09-11. www.spsg.de. Admission 12€ adults, 8€ concessions. Apr–Oct Tues–Sun 10am–6pm, closed Mon; Nov–Mar to 5pm. S-Bahn: Westend.*

❷ ★★★ kids Schlossgarten. Berliners come to jog, stroll, and relax in the sunshine within Schloss Charlottenburg's grounds. Laid out in 1697 in formal French baroque style by Siméon Godeau—a protégée of Le Nôtre, of Versailles fame—the landscaped park reveals petite summer palaces and River Spree views.

Gaze up at the Grossen Kurfürsten statue at Schloss Charlottenburg.

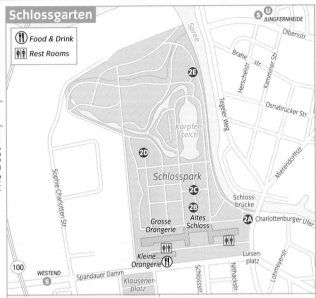

Schlossgarten

🍴 Food & Drink

🚻 Rest Rooms

Tucked behind the Schloss is the **2A Neue Pavillon,** built by the ubiquitous Prussian architect Karl Friedrich Schinkel for King Friedrich Wilhelm III in 1824. The summer palace is inspired by Neapolitan Villa Reale del Chiatamone, where the king stayed on his visit to Italy in 1822. When the pavilion reopens following renovation in late 2011, visitors will be able to view an exhibition of Biedermeier porcelain and paintings, including works by German Romantic painter Carl Blechen. Stroll the ornamental **2B Parterre,** planted with perennials, snapdragons, and irises. This leads to the **2C Carp Pond,** where I have my camera handy for a wide-screen view of the palace with the gardens in the foreground. Farther north, the

2D Mausoleum, a neoclassical, columned temple, harbors the ornate Carrara marble sarcophagus of Queen Luise of Prussia who died in 1810, and her beloved husband Friedrich William III, who departed 30 years later. Continue northeast to the riverfront to appreciate Carl Gotthard Langhans' bijou **2E Belvedere,** a 1788 rococo pavilion topped by a bronze cupola. Friedrich Wilhelm III used to enjoy tea and classical music here. Inside is a precious collection of porcelain by royal manufacturer KPM. 🕐 *1½ hr. Admission to gardens free; Belvedere 3€ adults, 2.50€concessions; Mausoleum 2€ adults, 1.50€ concessions. Gardens: daily 8am–dusk. Outer buildings Tues–Sun 10am–5pm. S-Bahn: Westend.*

3 ★★ Museum Berggruen.

Modern art fans shouldn't miss this impressive gallery housing the private collection of Heinz Berggruen (1914–2007), one of the most prolific German-born Jewish art collectors of the 20th century. The star attraction is his Picasso collection, showcasing around 100 works, from the artist's early sketches to expressive Blue

Period creations. Keep an eye out for the 1909 cubist masterpiece *Houses on the Hill*. Paul Klee originals, Henri Matisse paper-cuts, and Alberto Giacometti sculptures complement an exhibition that spans three floors. ⏲ *1 hr. Schlossstrasse 1.* ☎ *030-32-69-58-15. Admission 8€ adults, 4€ concessions, free for children under 18. Tues–Sun 10am–6pm, Mon closed. S-Bahn: Westend.*

④ ★ Bröhan Museum. Next door is another little-known gem: A temple to Berlin art dealer and collector Karl Bröhan's *Jugendstil* (Art Nouveau) and Art Deco treasures. The museum takes a chronological spin through interior design, emphasizing French and Belgian styles, from fine Meissen porcelain to Emile Gallé's exquisite glasswork. A fine array of Art Nouveau and Functionalist furniture by Henry van de Velde (1863–1957) and Josef Hoffmann (1870–1956) is also on display. The 1st-floor gallery presents pastels and paintings, including Berlin Secessionist works by Karl Hagemeister (1848–1933) and Walter Leistikow (1865–1908). ⏲ *45 min. Schlossstrasse 1a.* ☎ *030-32-69-06-00. www.broehan-museum.de. Admission 8€ adults, 4€ concessions, free for children under 18. Tues–Sun 10am–6pm, Mon closed. S-Bahn: Westend.*

⑤ Opera Italiana. Stop by this friendly Italian for good-value lunch dishes. Pizza, pasta, salads, and staples like pork medallions with mushrooms are on the menu. There's plenty to appeal to kids and vegetarians too. *Spandauer Damm 5.* ☎ *030-34-70-36-26. €–€€.*

⑥ ★★ Sammlung Scharf-Gerstenberg. Delve into the fantasy world of Surrealist masters like Dalí, Magritte, Goya, Max Ernst, and Paul Klee at this outstanding new Charlottenburg gallery. The former 19th-century royal stables of King Wilhelm IV have been transformed into a cutting-edge art space showing paintings, sculptures, and works on paper, as well as Surrealist film classics. There's also a cafe and bookstore on site. ⏲ *1 hr. Schlossstrasse 70.* ☎ *030-34-35-73-15. Admission 8€ adults, 4€ concessions, children under 18 free. Tues–Sat 10am–6pm, closed Mon. S-Bahn: Westend.*

⑦ ★ Schlossstrasse. Lined with grand villas, this leafy boulevard is perfect for a languid stroll through gentrified Charlottenburg. It was built in the 17th century (then called Breite Strasse, "wide street") with lodgings for royal servants. Near Schloss Charlottenburg, you can spot Eugen Boermel's bronze memorial to Prince Albert of Prussia (1809–72), a Prussian colonel general. In the late afternoon, locals often gather on the boulevard to play boules or walk their dogs. ⏲ *30 min. U-Bahn: Sophie-Charlotte-Platz.*

⑧ kids Schustehrus Park. A detour onto Schustehrusstrasse brings you to this quiet pocket of greenery, once the garden of Villa Oppenheim (see below). With its mature trees, herbaceous borders, and groomed lawns, it's a romantic park off the well-trodden tourist trail. There's also a small children's playground here. ⏲ *15 min. Schustehrusstrasse. U-Bahn: Sophie-Charlotte-Platz.*

⑨ Villa Oppenheim. At the time of writing, this beautiful late-19th-century, neo-Renaissance villa was being restored to its former glory. It's set to reopen in late 2011 and will show art from the Charlottenburg collection, including works by Berlin Secessionist Walter Leistikow (1865–1908) and German-Jewish Impressionist painter and etcher Max Liebermann (1847–1935). Call ahead for opening times. ⏲ *45 min. Schlossstrasse 55.* ☎ *030-902-91-67-04. Admission free. U-Bahn: Sophie-Charlotte-Platz.*

Potsdam

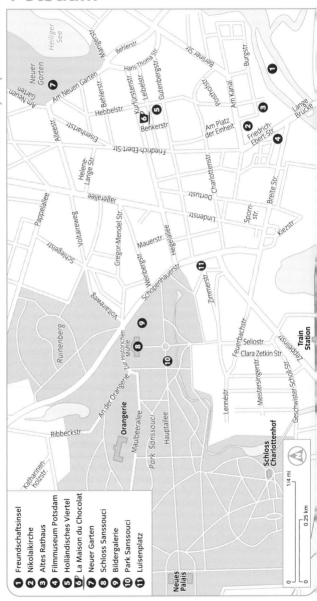

The Best Day Trips & Excursions

1. Freundschaftsinsel
2. Nikolaikirche
3. Altes Rathaus
4. Filmmuseum Potsdam
5. Holländisches Viertel
6. La Maison du Chocolat
7. Neuer Garten
8. Schloss Sanssouci
9. Bildergalerie
10. Park Sanssouci
11. Luisenplatz

Potsdam, capital of the Berlin-Brandenburg region and UNESCO World Heritage site, is just 24km (15 miles) southwest of Berlin. Within the space of a day you can time-travel to architecture inspired by Ancient Greece, glimpse Dutch gables in the Holländisches Viertel, and explore an English country garden. Potsdam's biggest asset, however, is Park Sanssouci for its baroque architecture.

START: 40-minute train journey from Berlin Hauptbahnhof to Potsdam.

1 kids Freundschaftsinsel.
Friendship Island hugging the banks of the River Havel is given over to a charming English-style garden. Start your day with a picnic breakfast under the willows shading the riverfront, or saunter among the flowery lawns where abstract bronze sculptures peep above the bushes. ⏱ *30 min. Lange Brücke. Admission free. Daily 7am–dusk.*

2 Nikolaikirche. You may be forgiven for thinking that you're in Italy while admiring this mighty neoclassical creation, completed in 1837 and inspired by Santa Maria Maggiore in Rome. Rising above a cobblestone square, the church is the handiwork of Karl Friedrich Schinkel (1781–1841), a prolific 19th-century German architect. Ascend the tower for a fine view over Potsdam. ⏱ *20 min. Am Alten Markt.* ☎ *0331-270-86-02. Admission free to the church; tower 5€. Daily 9am–5pm.*

3 Altes Rathaus. Next door, this Greco-Roman inspired town hall dating from the mid-18th century grabs your attention with its Corinthian colonnade and cherubs. Perched on top of the cupola is the mythological Greek Titan Atlas, bent under the weight of his globe. The Altes Rathaus was undergoing a complete makeover at the time of writing, and is set to open as a

museum showcasing local history in 2012. ⏱ *10 min. Am Alten Markt.*

4 ★ Filmmuseum Potsdam.
These former Prussian royal stables have lost none of their splendor, with an elongated baroque facade bearing the imprint of Sanssouci architect Knobelsdorff. The museum inside traces the history of the Babelsberg studios back to 1912—movie buffs are sure to love the collection of props, costumes, and film clips. ⏱ *45 min. Breite Strasse 1a.* ☎ *0331-271-81-12. www.filmmuseum-potsdam.de. Admission 3.50€ adults, 2€ concessions. Tues–Sun 10am–6pm, closed Mon.*

5 ★★ Holländisches Viertel.
Centered around Am Bassin and Benkerstrasse, the quaint Dutch Quarter is named after the Dutch craftsmen who came to Potsdam in the mid-18th century at the invitation of "Soldier King" Frederick Wilhelm I. As you wander the cobbled lanes past gabled houses, look for Am Bassin 10, where Mozart lived in 1789, and the Italianate belfry of nearby St. Peter und Paul Kirche (1870). Roam the antiques shops, boutiques, and galleries lining Benkerstrasse for everything from jewelry to hand-thrown pots. Stepping northwest, the neo-Gothic Nauener Tor (1755) is one of the last remaining city gates. ⏱ *45 min.*

Glimpse Atlas atop Potsdam's Altes Rathaus.

6 La Maison du Chocolat. On warm days, the terrace here is the best place to enjoy the Holländisches Viertel's Dutch ambiance. The old-world cafe is famed for its smooth hot chocolate and tarte aux pommes. *Benkertstrasse 20.* ☎ *0331-237-07-30. €–€€.*

7 ★★ kids Neuer Garten. This serene park hugs the banks of reed-fringed Heiliger See, a haven for wild birds. Although swimming is forbidden, you can occasionally spot plucky locals taking a dip. The gardens were laid out in 1787 in English landscape style with mature oaks and broad avenues. Seek out the Marmorpalais on the west bank, a fanciful redbrick and white marble confection built for King Friedrich Wilhelm II in 1787. Farther north stands **Schloss Cecilienhof**, an English mock-Tudor manor built in 1917 and where the Potsdam Agreement was signed in 1945, dividing postwar Germany into four occupied zones. ⏰ *1 hr.*

8 ★★★ Schloss Sanssouci. King Friedrich II of Prussia's whimsical summer palace is Potsdam's biggest visitor draw. Perched above terraced vineyards, the rococo

Rest by the fountain on Luisenplatz to admire the Brandenburg Gate.

creation was built in 1747 by Georg Wenzeslaus von Knobelsdorff as an escape for Friedrich from his courtly functions. The facade is graced with slender Corinthian columns and reliefs depicting the Roman god of wine, Bacchus. An audio guide in English or a 40-minute guided tour in German takes in state rooms such as the oval Marmorsaal, adorned with Tuscan Carrara marble and gold swirls, where the king entertained French philosopher Voltaire. The bookcases in the cedarwood library are lined with the leather-bound books of Greek and Roman academics. Back outside, a wander through terraced vineyards takes you to the 18m-high (59 ft.) Great Fountain, for picture-postcard views of the palace. Don't forget your camera. ⏰ *1 hr. Maulbeerallee.* ☎ *0331-969-42-00. www.spsg.de. Admission Apr–Oct 12€ adults, 8€ concessions; Nov–Mar 8€ adults, 5€ concessions. Apr–Oct Tues–Sun 10am–6pm; Nov–Mar to 5pm.*

9 ★★ Bildergalerie. Practically an extension of Schloss Sanssouci, this picture gallery's unassuming facade belies a sumptuous marble and gold interior. It harbors a magnificent collection of Old Master paintings, including works by baroque notable Peter Paul Rubens (1577–1640), errant Italian genius Caravaggio (1571–1610), and Flemish portrait artist Anthony van Dyck (1599–1641). Pick up a flyer in English detailing the most important works. ⏰ *45 min. Park Sanssouci 4.* ☎ *0331-969-41-81. Admission 3€ adults, 2.50€ concessions. May–Oct Tues–Sun 10am–6pm.*

10 ★★★ kids Park Sanssouci. Thinking that hunting was barbaric and unworthy of a king, Frederick introduced elements of fantasy and intrigue into his baroque backyard.

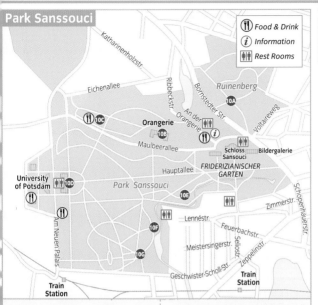

Park Sanssouci

Food & Drink
Information
Rest Rooms

First up is the 19th-century **A Sizilianischer Garten** (Sicilian Garden), where you wander past myrtles and laurels to the Italian Renaissance-inspired **B Orangerie** (1864). Take time to appreciate the villa's towers and arcades. Inside, the crowd-pullers are 50 copies of paintings by Italian Renaissance master Raphael Sanzio (1483–1520). Soon you're drawn to the dragons that crown the pagoda-style **C Drachenhaus** (1770), now housing a restaurant. Head along the tree-fringed Hauptallee to the Prussian **D Neues Palais,** a baroque palace embellished with a monumental cupola; being a modest fellow,

Friedrich favored his smaller pad, Schloss Sanssouci. Equally enchanting is Johann Gottfried Büring's **E Chinesisches Teehaus** (1764), an exquisite turquoise pavilion graced with life-size gold figurines sipping tea and merrymaking. Farther south are Karl Friedrich Schinkel's **F Römische Bäder** (1829), which recall a 15th-century Italian country house with an open arcade and bathhouse. Nearby **G Schloss Charlottenhof** (1829) is modeled on a Roman villa. ⏱ *1½ hr. Admission free to gardens; day pass covering all attractions including Schloss Sanssouci and Bildergalerie 15€ adults, 10€ concessions.*

11 kids Luisenplatz. Locals gather by the fountain in this monumental square, overshadowed by the triumphal arch of Brandenburger Tor built in 1770 by prolific German architect Carl von Gontard, who also worked on Park Sanssouci, and his talented apprentice Georg

Christian Unger. On the other side of the gate is Brandenburger Strasse, a pedestrianized thoroughfare fringed by high-street shops and alfresco cafes. From here, the station to take you back to Berlin is just a 10-minute stroll. ⏱ *15 min.*

Tropical Islands

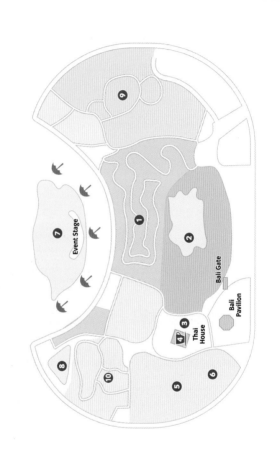

1 Rainforest
2 Balinese Lagoon
3 Tropical Village
4 Jabarimba
5 Tropino Club
6 African Jungle Lift
7 Tropical Sea
8 Waterslide Tower
9 Spa & Sauna
10 Rainforest Camp

Tropical Islands rises above the pine-wooded Spreewald, 60km (37 miles) south of Berlin. It's the world's highest free-standing hall, originally intended as a Zeppelin hangar. Add a rainforest, lagoon, and beaches and you have the perfect indoor water wonderland. When temperatures dip below zero, Berliners flock to this former airbase to sip margaritas under the palms. START: **Train to Brand (Niederlausitz).**

① ★★ **kids Rainforest.** At the heart of Tropical Islands is the world's largest indoor rainforest, nurturing more than 50,000 tropical plants and trees. Veer right after the entrance onto a trail that twists past lush banana and jackfruit trees, coffee bushes, and carnivorous plants. It's quite something to find yourself under a canopy of palms and ferns, where crickets chirp and flowers scent the air. Take note of rare orchid species and fragrant ylang-ylang trees. The footpath emerges at a mangrove swamp, featuring a cascading waterfall and turtles dozing on the rocks.

② ★ **Balinese Lagoon.** The sugar-white sands and 32°C (90°F) waters at this themed lagoon transport you all the way to Bali. Bathers can drift in a kidney-shaped pool, duck under waterfalls streaking the cliff faces, or catch rays on the beach. Make sure you slap on the sunscreen, because UV rays penetrate the transparent foil roof. Let the whirlpools, bubble-jet loungers, and a lazy river pummel you into relaxation.

③ **kids Tropical Village.** The village is the resort's main shopping and dining drag. Passing through a Balinese temple gate brings you to a re-created Thai teak house (fashioned by Ladda Teijavnaija, architect to the Thai royals), a thatched Samoan *fale* (house), and a Borneo longhouse. You can also find snack bars and restaurants, serving everything from crepes to Thai curry.

④ **Jabarimba.** This international restaurant inside the teak house is your best bet for a tropical barbecue lunch. Choose steak or fresh fish, pick a marinade, and watch it sizzle on a hot stone. DJs spin tunes in the cocktail lounge after dark. €€.

⑤ **kids Tropino Club.** The Jolly Roger flies high at this kids club, where tots can play freely on the pirate ship and gigantic climbing frames, shoot foam balls, and zip around the go-kart track. Occasionally Urmel the dragon makes an appearance. Young children must be accompanied by an adult. *Daily 10:30am–9pm.*

Relax under the waterfalls in the 32°C Balinese Lagoon.

Practical Matters

Tropical Islands is open 24 hours a day, 365 days a year. Entry costs 28.50€ for adults and 23€ for children under 14; it costs an extra 15€ to crash overnight on a sunlounger. Visitors are issued with a chip wristband, which can be used to pay for treatments and snacks. Settle your account when you leave; major credit cards are accepted. Trains depart roughly every hour from Berlin Hauptbahnhof to Brand (Niederlausitz); the journey takes between 55 and 80 minutes and costs 7.80€. From here there are free shuttle buses. For more information, contact Tropical Islands on ☎ 0354-77-60-50-50 or see www.tropical-islands.de.

6 ★ kids African Jungle Lift. Buried in the jungle, the latest attraction at Tropical Islands is one for thrill-seekers. Be hauled up to 20m (67 ft.) on a giant tree trunk before plummeting to ground level in one single stomach-churning drop. There is a great, albeit fleeting, view of the complex from the top. *Children under 1.2m (4 ft.) must be accompanied by an adult. Admission 3.50€ per day. Daily 11am–9pm.*

7 ★★★ kids Tropical Sea. The dimensions of this indoor ocean are head-spinning. An enormous cloudy sky forms a surreal backdrop to a "sea" the size of four Olympic swimming pools. The azure 28°C (82°F) water here is slightly cooler than the lagoon, so better for swimming laps. Kids can splash in the adjacent shallow pool or build sandcastles on the beach. Acrobats, magicians, and dancers entertain the crowds nightly on the Island Stage after dark.

8 kids Waterslide Tower. This trio of waterslides is strictly for thrill-seekers. Scariest is the white-knuckle Blue Slide, Germany's highest at 25m (82 ft.) where you might pick up speeds of 70km/h (43 miles/h). *Admission 3.50€ per day. Daily 9am–1am.*

9 ★★★ Spa & Sauna. You need to leave your modesty behind to get into this nudist-only wellness area. It's worth the blushes to steam in the natural earth sauna of the basalt Alcantara Canyon, inhale herbal aromas in the Jungle Village, and then head over to the temple-like mist cavern at Angkor Wat. The Elefanta Temple is based on Mumbai's famous caves and offers a foot spa, Ayurvedic treatments, and a sauna glittering with amethyst and rose quartz. Waiotapu recreates New Zealand's thermal landscape with soothing geysers and hot springs. *Entry an additional 8.50€ not including treatments. Daily 9am–1am.*

10 ★ kids Rainforest Camp. Feel like spending the night in this indoor jungle? If you want more comfort than a lounger on the beach, this palm-fringed campsite makes the best base. Teepees are equipped with mattresses and bed linen, and guests can use the shared shower blocks. Booking ahead is essential. An overnight stay entitles you to free admission to Tropical Islands the next day. *Overnight stay 24.50€ per person.* ●

The
Savvy Traveler

Before You Go

Government Tourist Offices

For pre-travel enquiries, contact **Visit Berlin** (Am Karlsbad 11; www. visitberlin.de). Their website has information in English to help plan your stay and you can order maps and brochures online. Their **call center** (☎ 030-25-00-25) deals with accommodation bookings.
German National Tourist Offices: In the U.S.: 122 East 42nd Street, Suite 2000, New York, NY 10168-0072 (☎ 212/661-7200; www. cometogermany.com). **In Canada:** 2 Bloor St West, Suite 2601, Toronto, M4W 3E2 (☎ 416/935-1896). **In the U.K.:** PO Box 2695, London W1A 3TN (☎ 020/317-09-08; www.germany-tourism.co.uk).

The Best Times to Go

Every season has its appeal, but **May** through **August** are the most popular months, when the weather warms and locals flock to the city's gardens, lidos, and beaches. Even in peak months, temperatures rarely exceed 30°C (86°F). Summer is also best for music festivals, open-air screenings, and beer garden jaunts, though beds can be scarce so book well ahead. **September** and **October** are cooler and quieter—with fewer crowds, and reductions on hotels and airfares up for grabs. **November's** great cultural lineup enlivens the dull onset of winter. Although **December** can be bitingly cold, it offers winter warmers at its **Christmas** markets. Wintry weather continues through to March, with the thermometer often dipping below freezing in **January** and **February.**

Festivals & Special Events

SPRING. Classical music lovers descend on Berlin for the 10-day

MaerzMusik festival (www.berliner festspiele.de) in March, staging contemporary orchestral and chamber works, including several premières. The immensely popular **Festtage (Festival Days)** strike a chord at Easter with gala concerts and operas at Staatsoper Unter den Linden. May 1 means **May Day** rallies, particularly in the Kreuzberg and Prenzlauer Berg districts. Rioting is not uncommon, so it's wise to give these neighborhoods a wide berth.

SUMMER. Kreuzberg celebrates the **Carnival of Cultures** (www. karneval-berlin.de; p 71) in June with parades, club nights, and plenty of hip-wiggling in the streets.
Feel the pride at the **Christopher Street Day** parade (www. csd-berlin.de) in late June, when gay and lesbian revelers turn out for a flamboyant street party between Kurfürstendamm and Siegessäule. Watch romantic flicks and big screen classics under the stars at Kreuzberg's **Open-air Cinema** (www.freiluftkino-kreuzberg.de) from May to August. Following Paris's lead, Berlin leaps into summer with the free **Fête de la Musique** (www.fetedelamusique.de) in June; it's a mammoth street music festival with everything from choirs to DJs rocking the city on 60 stages. The focus switches to classical symphonies on elegant Gendarmenmarkt for **Classic Open Air Berlin** (www. classicopenair.de) in July, whereas dance takes center stage at the dynamic **Tanz im August** festival (www.tanzimaugust.de) in August. Berlin rivals Munich in the beer-guzzling and pretzel-munching stakes with its very own *August-fest*—the **Berlin International**

Beer Festival (www.bierfestival-berlin.de; p 22). Grab a stein to join the swaying crowds on Karl-Marx-Allee, for beer tents, live bands, and merrymaking. Need a cultural fix? Head over for the **Long Night of Museums** in August, when 100 museums and galleries stay open late and host special events.

FALL. September's **Berlin Literary Festival** (www.literaturfestival.com) rustles up a feast of poetry and fiction, accompanied by free concerts, readings, and screenings. For a less highbrow event, try **Popkomm** (www.popkomm.com), a gigantic music and clubbing festival, featuring 3 days of electric beats and up-and-coming talent at venues across Berlin. Later in the month the **Berlin Marathon** (www.real-berlin-marathon.com) comes to town; the 42km (26.2 miles) track takes in landmarks from Siegessäule to Unter den Linden. On **Tag der Deutschen Einheit** (Oct 3), a huge street party celebrates German reunification with events from live music to cabaret taking place around the Reichstag and Brandenburg Gate. As the days draw in, Berlin's **Festival of Lights** brightens up the season with dazzling projections on landmarks from Unter den Linden to Alexanderplatz. In early November, Berlin hosts **JazzFest** (www.berlinerfestspiele.de), when soloists and swinging quartets hit stages across the city.

WINTER. Ideal for children, the **Berlin Fairytale Days Festival** in November welcomes authors and storytellers to Berlin. 'Tis the season to drink cinnamon-laced *Glühwein* (mulled wine), chomp on gingerbread, and get giddy on the carrousels at Berlin's **Weihnachtsmärkte** (Christmas markets) in December. **Gendarmenmarkt** (www.gendarmenmarktberlin.de) is particularly enchanting with a twinkling tree and traditional gifts such as hand-carved nutcrackers and toys. Acrobats, jugglers, and choirs keep shoppers amused. Twirl across the ice rink or race down the toboggan run at the glittering **Winterwelt** (www.winterwelt-berlin.de) on Potsdamer Platz from November to early January. Fireworks, parties, and open-air concerts ring in the **New Year** (http://silvester-berlin.de) at the Brandenburg Gate. The small but innovative **Britspotting** festival (www.britspotting.de) attracts aficionados of British independent film to Kino Babylon in late January. A big event on the media arts calendar in early February is **Transmediale** (www.transmediale.de) at the Haus der Kulturen der Welt. In February, film buffs are glued to big screens, as the **Berlinale** (www.berlinale.de) draws the cream of the cinematic world to Berlin.

The Weather

Part of Berlin's year-round appeal is its continental climate, characterized by cool winters and warm (but not stiflingly hot) summers. In spring, temperatures hit highs of around 18°C (64°F). Summer spells sunshine and temperatures hovering around 25°C (77°F), which means air conditioning in hotel rooms is a luxury rather than a necessity. Berlin's parks are ablaze with color in September and October, but expect chillier days (2–10°C/35–50°F). Winters are cold, particularly when an icy wind blows from Russia, with temperatures often plummeting below freezing from December to February. Whichever season you choose, pack layers because Berlin's weather can be fickle and showers spontaneous, even in midsummer.

BERLIN'S AVERAGE TEMPERATURE & RAINFALL

	JAN	FEB	MAR	APR	MAY	JUNE
Daily Temp. (°F)	34	36	41	49	58	63
Daily Temp. (°C)	1	2	5	9.5	14.5	17.5
Rainfall (in.)	3.3	3.1	3.1	2.3	3.5	4.7
Rainfall (cm)	8.4	7.9	7.9	5.8	8.9	11.9

	JULY	AUG	SEPT	OCT	NOV	DEC
Daily Temp. (°F)	67	67	59	50	41	35
Daily Temp. (°C)	19.5	19.5	15	10.5	5	1.5
Rainfall (in.)	4.8	3.9	3.5	2.7	3.2	3
Rainfall (cm)	12.2	9.9	8.9	6.8	8.1	7.6

Useful Websites

- **www.bahn.co.uk**: Deutsche Bahn (German Rail) site for routes, schedules, and ticket booking.
- **www.berlin.de**: Comprehensive information about Berlin, including culture, transport, and politics.
- **www.berlin.info**: English-language site on Berlin; themes stretch from arts and culture to food and drink.
- **www.bvg.de**: Berlin's official public transport site with timetables, routes, maps, and an online journey planner.

Cell (Mobile) Phones

Cell phones are referred to locally as *Handys*. Like the rest of Europe, Berlin operates on the GSM 900/1800 network, compatible with Australian and other World Phones. Call your operator to activate roaming and ensure the international call bar is unlocked. Check charges, because they can be high. If your cell phone doesn't work in Germany, invest in a local GSM phone with a prepaid SIM card (around 30€ total) for affordable calling rates. A central store is **Vodafone** (Friedrichstrasse 90; ☎ 0173-205-00-61; www.vodafone. de). North Americans can rent a GSM phone before leaving home from **RoadPost** (☎ 888/290-1606 or 905/272-4934; www.roadpost. com). In the UK, try **Cellhire** (☎ 01904-616-810).

Car Rentals

Driving in Berlin is hassle-free compared with other European cities of a similar size. If you're staying in the center, however, it's quicker and easier to get around using the speedy public transport network. All major international car-rental companies operate here, with branches at the airports, Hauptbahnhof, and in the center. Among them are **Avis** (☎ 800/331-1212; www.avis.com), **Hertz** (☎ 800/654-3001; www.hertz.com), and **Budget** (☎ 800/472-3325; www.budget. com). Reputable agencies include **Holiday Autos** (☎ 866/392-92-88; www.holidayautos.com), and **Auto Europe** (☎ 800/223-55-55; www. autoeurope.com).

Getting **There**

By Plane

Until the new Berlin-Brandenburg International Airport opens in 2012, two airports serve Berlin: **Tegel** (TXL) and **Schönefeld** (SXF). See www.berlin-airport.de for up-to-date information on all Berlin's airports, or call ☎ 0180-5000-186.

Tegel airport (8km/5 miles northwest of the center) serves European and long-haul destinations. Continental Airlines operate daily nonstop flights to Newark Liberty International Airport and Delta Airlines to JFK Airport in New York. Major European airlines serving Tegel include British Airways to London Heathrow, KLM to Amsterdam, and Air France with flights to Paris. **Buses** 128, X9, 109, and the **Jet Express TXL** depart for Berlin from stops outside the terminal every 10 or 20 minutes from 6am to 11pm. The journey takes between 15 and 40 minutes; tickets cost 2.30€ and can be purchased at the BVG kiosk close to the airport exit or from the ticket machines at the bus station. Validate your ticket by stamping it in the machine on the bus. A **taxi** ride will set you back around 25€; taxis depart from ranks outside the terminal.

Schönefeld airport (18km/11 miles southeast of the center) connects with destinations across Europe, Asia, and Africa, and is served by low-cost airlines like easyJet, Ryanair, and Germanwings. A regular **S-Bahn** service (S45 and S9) departs from the airport and takes roughly 45 minutes to reach central Berlin. Alternatively take the **Airport Express** train, departing every half-hour from 4:30am to 11pm and taking 28 minutes to reach Hauptbahnhof, stopping en route at Ostbahnhof, Alexanderplatz, and Friedrichstrasse. Tickets for either service cost 3€ and can be purchased from the machines on the platforms. Expect to pay around 35€ for the 45-minute **taxi** journey into town.

By Car

The **A10** highway orbits the city, linking Berlin to the rest of Germany and Europe. The **A11** leads northeast to Szczecin in Poland and the **A13** drops south to Dresden. Hop on the **A9** highway for major German cities farther south of Berlin including Leipzig, Bayreuth, Nuremberg, and Munich. The **A2** leads west to Hanover and the **A24** northwest to Hamburg. On the ring road, look out for signs into central Berlin: Take the **A115** for the west, the **A113** for the southeast, and the **A114** for the north of the city. German highways are speed limit-free unless otherwise indicated, but you should watch your speed in built-up areas, because there's usually a 30km/h (18 miles/h) or 50km/h (30 miles/h) limit.

By Train

National and international trains—including Deutsche Bahn InterCity-Express (ICE), InterCity (IC), EuroCity (EC), InterRegio (IR), and overnight City Night Line trains with comfortable sleeper carriages —chug into the **Hauptbahnhof**, Europaplatz (☎ 118-61). Berlin's ultramodern central station links long-distance trains with local S-Bahn and U-Bahn services. **Deutsche Bahn** (DB) is Germany's state-owned railway company. For comprehensive information on routes, timetables, fares, and ticket booking, see their English-language website (www.bahn.co.uk). Tickets can also be booked

City Savers

You can save euros on sightseeing with one of Berlin's discount cards. The WelcomeCard and Museum Pass are available online at www.visitberlin.de and at Berlin Infostores (p 172).

Berlin WelcomeCard Covers public transport in zones AB and gives reductions on some 160 sights and attractions. A 48-hour, 72-hour, 5-day pass costs 16.90€/22.90€/29.90€. A 72-hour pass including admission to Museum Island's galleries and museums costs 34€.

Museum Pass This 3-day Berlin pass costs 19€ (9.50€ concessions) and provides access to 60 museums across the city, including most of those mentioned in this book.

Berlin CityTourCard A variation of the WelcomeCard, this money-saving card gives you unlimited use of public transport (zones AB) and substantial discounts on sights, attractions, tours, theaters, shops and bars. A 48-hour, 72-hour, 5-day pass costs 15.90€/21.90€/28.90€. It is sold at airports and major train stations including Berlin Hauptbahnhof, Zoologischer Garten and Alexanderplatz. See www.citytourcard.com for more details.

by calling their hotline (☎ 08718-80-80-66). If you are traveling long distances, consider purchasing the **German Rail Pass,** which allows you to travel on all high-speed trains in Germany and takes you as far as Salzburg, Austria, and Basel, Switzerland. You can choose from 3 to 10 days in a month; a 3-day pass starts at 175€. Visit the Deutsche Bahn website for details on discount schemes and passes such as Inter-Rail and BahnCard.

By Bus
Most long-distance buses pull into the **Zentraler Omnibusbahnhof/ ZOB** (Masurenallee 4–6; ☎ 030-861-93 -31), opposite the Funkturm in Charlottenburg. The station links Berlin to 350 destinations across Germany and Europe. Companies operating to/from here include **Eurolines** (www.eurolines.com), **EuroTouring** (www.eurotouring. de), and **BerlinLinienBus** (www. berlinlinienbus.de).

Getting **Around**

By S-Bahn
Speedy and efficient, **S-Bahn** suburban trains (☎ 030-29-74-33-33; www.s-bahn-berlin.de) are one of the most enjoyable ways to explore Berlin and its suburbs. The service comprises 15 routes, which feed into three main lines: The east–west

Stadtbahn, the north–south *Nord–Süd Bahn*, and the circular *Ring-bahn*. Purchase and validate your ticket at one of the red or yellow stamping machines at the platform before boarding. Berlin is divided into three **tariff zones:** AB (2.30€), BC (2.70€), and ABC (3€). A single

AB ticket suffices for most journeys; if you're planning more than two trips, invest in a day pass (6.30€–6.80€). The S-Bahn operates from 4am to 12:30am, later at weekends.

By U-Bahn

Operating on the same fare system as the S-Bahn, **U-Bahn** underground trains (☎ 030-19-44-9; www.bvg.de) are another means of getting around Berlin, though they generally stop more frequently. Ten lines run to more than 170 stations from 4am until midnight, later at the weekend. At peak times, services depart every 3 to 5 minutes.

By Bus

If you're not in a hurry, Berlin's **buses** can be a great way to get about and enjoy the views, especially from the upper deck; routes 100 and 200 are particularly scenic (p 13). Although services are plentiful—150 day and 54 night routes—they can be painfully slow during rush hour. Ticket prices are the same as those for the S-Bahn and U-Bahn. Download routes from www.bvg.de or for information call ☎ 030-19-44-9.

By Taxi

Taxis wait outside major hotels, stations, and airports round the clock. Most drivers speak some English. There is a minimum charge of 3.20€, plus 1.65€ per kilometer. If you are going less than 2km (1.2 miles) and flag the taxi down on the street, you can ask for the *Kurzstreckentarif* (short-route fare); the driver should switch off the meter and charge no more than 4€ for the ride. Reputable companies include **TaxiFunk Berlin GmbH** (☎ 030-44-33-22) and **Funk Taxi Berlin** (☎ 030-26-10-26). Note that fares may be higher when roads are busy.

By Car

Once in central Berlin, there's little need for a **car**; it's cheaper, quicker, and more carbon friendly to use the excellent public transport network, even for day trips to Wannsee (p 100) and Potsdam (p 157) (by S-Bahn). If you are driving, however, you'll find Berlin easy to navigate thanks to clear signage and the ring road. Pay-and-display parking costs around 2€ per hour from 9am to 6pm or 8pm. Few machines accept credit cards, so have some change handy. Clearly display your ticket on the dash.

If you're staying for more than a few days, make use of Berlin's free **park and ride** service (www.vbbonline.de). These unsupervised car parks are connected to the center by S-Bahn or U-Bahn.

By Bicycle

Berlin's terrific network of **cycling** trails makes pedal-pushing popular. Bikes are a fun, eco-friendly way of exploring the sights. Most S-Bahn and U-Bahn trains have a dedicated compartment, but you need to buy a reduced fare ticket for your bike, which costs 1.50€ single or 4.50€ for a day pass in zone AB. To hire your own set of reliable wheels, check out **Fat Tire Bike Tours** (p 60). **Fahrradstation** (☎ 0180-510-80-00; www.fahrradstation.com) is another option with six outlets in the city. Expect to pay 15€–30€ per day. The 24-hour **Deutsche Bahn call a bike** service (☎ 0700-05-22-55-22; www.callbike.de) is convenient. Simply dial the number to receive a code that unlocks the bike. Rates are 0.08€ per minute and 12€ for 24 hours.

On Foot

Berlin's parks, squares, and waterways make **walking** a pleasure, especially in Tiergarten, Unter den

Linden, and the pedestrianized streets of the Nikolaiviertel. A leisurely stroll along the River Spree or Landwehrkanal is an excellent (and free) way of keeping fit and seeing the sights. If you want to cover more ground or your time is limited, cycling may be a better option.

Fast **Facts**

APARTMENT RENTALS Check out www.all-berlin-apartments.com, www.ferienwohnung-24-berlin.com, and www.apartmentsapart.com for modern holiday apartments and flats in Berlin, which are often remarkably good value for longer stays.

ATMS There are plenty of ATMs for withdrawing cash 24/7. Maestro, Cirrus, and Visa cards are widely accepted, but be aware that your bank may charge a fee for the service. You can exchange currency at banks, post offices, or EuroChange/Travelex offices at airports, Hauptbahnhof, and in Alexanderplatz.

BANKING HOURS Banks open 8:30am–4pm Monday through Friday. Office hours are usually Monday–Thursday from around 8/9am up to 6pm; many close at midday on Friday. Most major department stores open Monday through Saturday from 10am to 8pm, plus six Sundays throughout the year.

CONSULATES & EMBASSIES **U.S. Embassy,** Clayallee 170 (☎ 030-83-05-0); **Canadian Embassy,** Leipziger Platz 17 (☎ 030-20-31-20); **British Embassy,** Wilhelmstrasse 70–71 (☎ 030-20-45-70); **Australian Embassy,** Wallstrasse 76–79 (☎ 030-88-00-880); **New Zealand Embassy,** Friedrichstrasse 60 (☎ 030-20-62-10); **Irish Embassy,** Friedrichstrasse 200 (☎ 030-22-07-20).

DOCTORS Call ☎ 01804-22-55-23-62 to find an English-speaking doctor. The *Yellow Pages* lists medical specialists.

ELECTRICITY Germany uses 230 volts AC (50 cycles). European two-pin plugs are standard.

EMERGENCIES For ambulance or fire service, dial ☎ 112. See "Doctors," above, and "Police," below.

GAY & LESBIAN TRAVELERS Liberal Berlin makes no secret of being one of the gay capitals of the world. The city is a magnet to the international gay (*schwul*) and lesbian (*lesbisch*) community, with an unrivaled nightlife scene in its bars and clubs. If you need proof that Berlin embraces homosexuality, look no further than the city's openly gay mayor Klaus Wowereit, or the Christopher Street Day parade (p 164). Resources for gay travelers include **www.gayberlin4u.com** and **www.out-in-berlin.com**, with information in English.

HOLIDAYS German public holidays include: January 1 (New Year's Day), January 6 (Epiphany), March/April (Good Friday and Easter Monday), May 1 (May Day), May (Ascension), May/June (Whit Monday and Corpus Christi), August 15 (Assumption), October 3 (German Unity Day), October 31 (Reformation Day), November 1 (All Saints' Day), Wednesday before 23 November (Repentance Day), December 8 (Feast of the Immaculate Conception), December 25 (Christmas Day), and December 26 (St. Stephen's Day).

INSURANCE With a valid **European Health Insurance Card** (EHIC), EU citizens receive free or reduced-cost emergency health care in Germany. All travelers should have an adequate insurance policy before visiting, which covers cancelation, lost luggage, and car rental insurance. Try the following in the U.S.: **Access America** (☎ 866/284-8300; www.accessamerica.com); **Travel Guard International** (☎ 800/826-4919; www.travelguard.com); **Travel Insured International** (☎ 800/243-3174; www.travelinsured.com); and **Travelex Insurance Services** (☎ 800/228-9792; www.travelex-insurance.com). In the U.K., try **MoneySupermarket** (☎ 0845/345-5708; www.moneysupermarket.com).

For additional medical insurance, contact **MEDEX Assistance** (☎ 800/537-2029; www.medexassist.com) or **Global Rescue** (☎ 800/381-9754; www.globalrescue.com).

INTERNET You'll find Internet cafes doubling as discount call centers around major stations such as Zoologischer Garten; many offer a cheap, speedy connection (around 1€ per 30 min. online) and services such as Skype, printing, and faxing. A growing number of cafes, bars, and hotels now offer Wi-Fi (sometimes free to customers). The **Sony Center** (p 89) is a free Wi-Fi hotspot. For a list of other free hotspots, visit **www.hotspot-locations.de**.

LOST PROPERTY If your wallet has been lost or stolen, call your credit card company immediately and file a report at the nearest police station. There's one near Alexanderplatz (Keibelstrasse 32; ☎ 030-4664-332-700).

Visa's toll-free emergency number in the U.S. is ☎ 800/847-2911, or 0800-811-8440 in Germany. **American Express** cardholders and traveler's check holders should call ☎ 888/412-6945 in the U.S. or 0800-101-23-62 in Germany. **MasterCard** holders should call ☎ 800/627-8372 in the U.S. or 0800-819-1040 in Germany.

MAIL & POSTAGE Deutsche Post (☎ 0180-233-33; www.deutschepost.de) provide postal services in Germany. Post offices are identified by a yellow sign with a black horn. Most open from 8:30am–6:30pm Monday through Friday, and Saturday 8:30am–noon. Central branches include Friedrichstrasse 69, Europaplatz, and Alexanderplatz 1.

Here are the international prices for stamps: Postcard 0.75€; standard letter under 20g 0.75€; letter under 50g 1.45€; letter under 500g 3.45€; package under 2kg 16.90€.

MONEY Germany's currency is the **euro.** At the time of writing, the exchange rate was approximately 1€ = \$1.35 (or £0.84). For up-to-date rates, check the currency converter website **www.xe.com**.

PASSPORTS & VISAS EU, U.S., Canadian, and Australian visitors must have a valid passport to enter Germany, but don't require a visa for stays of fewer than 90 days. It's advisable to keep a separate photocopy of your passport. If your passport is lost or stolen, contact your embassy (see "Consulates & Embassies," above).

PHARMACIES Pharmacies (*Apotheken*) operate during normal business hours and post details of the nearest 24-hour pharmacy; at least one per district stays open all night. Central pharmacies include **Pluspunkt Apotheke,** Friedrichstrasse 60 (☎ 030-20-16-61-73) and **Apotheke Berlin Hauptbahnhof** (☎ 030-20-61-41-90). Call ☎ 22-833 for the emergency pharmacy service. The website **www.berlin.de** lists pharmacies by district.

POLICE The national police emergency number is ☎ 110. For local police, dial ☎ 030-46-64-0.

SAFETY Overall, Berlin is a safe city. The usual commonsense rules apply: Keep an eye on your possessions in crowded tourist areas and don't walk alone at night. Pickpockets operate on the U-Bahn, so have your wits about you. You can alert the stationmaster by pushing the emergency "SOS" button. Though rare, extreme right-wing groups can turn violent toward people they consider "foreign." This is more prevalent in former East Berlin districts such as Lichtenberg and Marzahn-Hellersdorf.

SALES TAX & VAT See "Taxes," below.

SENIOR TRAVELERS Mention that you are a senior when making bookings and reservations. As in most German cities, people over the age of 65 qualify for reduced admission (20%–50%) to theaters and museums, and reduced fares on public transport. You may be asked to show ID.

SMOKING The *Nichtrauch-erschutzgesetz* (Non-Smokers' Protection Law) introduced in January 2008 means Berlin is in practice a smoke-free city, though in theory smoking is still allowed in certain establishments (particularly bars). Officially, smoking is banned in public places including on transport, and in offices, hospitals, and restaurants. If in doubt, ask.

TAXES Sales tax, Value added tax (VAT), or *Mehrwertsteuer* (MwSt) in German, ranges from 7% to 19%. Food and necessities are taxed at 7%, luxury goods (jewelry, tobacco, liquors) at 19%. Non-EU residents are entitled to a refund of the 19% MwSt tax if goods are exported within 3 months of purchase. The store provides you with forms, which you should have stamped at Customs on departure. For further details see **www.global-blue.com**.

TELEPHONES Call ☎ 11837 for national and ☎ 11834 for international directory enquiries. If you're making an international call, dial ☎ 00, wait for the tone, and dial the country code, area code, and number. To make a local call, dial the three-digit city prefix (**030** in Berlin), followed by the number.

TIPPING Restaurants add a service charge to the bill. If you are satisfied, a tip of 5% to 10% is standard on top of the service charge. Round up the bill to the nearest euro if it's just a coffee or snack. It's customary to tip your waiter/waitress when settling the bill, not by leaving money on the table. Tip hotel porters and doormen 1€ and maids about the same per day. A 10% tip is normal for taxi drivers. Keep spare change handy for washroom attendants.

TOILETS Berlin has a number of clean public toilets, many of them automatic and wheelchair-accessible. You need around 0.50€ to unlock the door.

TOURIST INFORMATION The multilingual staff at **BERLIN infostores** can provide information on sightseeing, help with ticket and tour bookings, and make hotel reservations. Central tourist offices include those at **Hauptbahnhof** (Europaplatz), open daily 8am to 10pm, the **Brandenburg Gate** (Pariser Platz), open daily 10am to 7pm, and the **Neuen Kranzler Eck** (Kurfürstendamm 22), open Monday through Saturday 10am–8pm and Sunday 9:30am–6pm.

Save on Culture

One of the best bargains in Berlin is the Berlin museum pass costing 19€ (9.50€ concessions) and providing access to 60 museums across the city over 3 days. Purchase the pass online at www. berlin-tourist-information.de or at a Berlin Infostore (p 172).

TRAVELERS WITH DISABILITIES Berlin is constantly improving public buildings to cater for *Behinderte* (people with disabilities). Many modern hotels, attractions, and restaurants are now wheelchair-friendly; some display a yellow **Berlin barrierefrei** (barrier-free Berlin) sign. Public transport network maps pinpoint stations equipped with ramps or elevators for easy access to the platforms. **Mobidat** (☎ 030-74-77-71-15; www.mobidat.net) has comprehensive information on accessible buildings and facilities in Berlin. A 24-hour hotline provides a **Wheelchair breakdown** service (☎ 0180-111-47-47). Deutsche Bahn offers an excellent service for travelers with special needs, including a 50% reduction on tickets and staff to assist at stations; for details contact the **Mobility Service Center** (☎ 01805-512-512; www.bahn.de). **Access-Able Travel Source** (☎ 303-232-2979; www.access-able.com) has access information for people traveling to Berlin.

Berlin: **A Brief History**

1237 Cölln, Berlin's sister town, is first mentioned in writing. The two cities merge for political and security reasons in 1307 and continue their rapid development.

1244 Berlin is founded as a trading post.

1307 Berlin and Cölln are united politically to form modern Berlin.

1415 Berlin comes under the rule of the Hohenzollern dynasty, the ruling house of Brandenburg-Prussia, which held sway until 1918. Friedrich I becomes the Elector of the Margraviate of Brandenburg, which he rules until 1440.

1451 Berlin becomes the royal residence of the Brandenburg electors and renounces its status as a free Hanseatic city.

1539 Berlin embraces Lutheran (Protestant) religious reform.

1576 Bubonic plague claims around 4,000 victims in Berlin.

1618–48 The Thirty Years' War reaps havoc. Berlin loses half its population in bloody religious and political feuds; the city is left devastated.

1647 Unter den Linden boulevard is constructed and planted with lime trees, on the orders of Frederick William of Brandenburg, to link Tiergarten to the Prussian palace (Schloss Hohenzollern).

1685 Edict of Potsdam. Frederick William gives the Calvinist Huguenots free passage to Brandenburg-Prussia following their expulsion from France. More than 6,000 settle in Berlin.

1695–99 Schloss Charlottenburg is built as a summer palace for Sophie Charlotte, the wife of Friedrich III, Elector of Brandenburg.

1701 The Elector Friedrich III is crowned king. Berlin becomes the capital of the Kingdom of Prussia. His grand plans include extending Schloss Charlottenburg in the style of the Palace of Versailles, outside Paris.

1740–86 Berlin flourishes as a center of the Enlightenment under Friedrich II of Prussia. He redesigns the city together with his favorite architect, Georg Wenzeslaus von Knobelsdorff; notable landmarks include Schloss Sanssouci.

1806–08 French Emperor Napoleon Bonaparte conquers Berlin, but grants the city self-government.

1810 The Humboldt University is founded by the Prussian educational reformer and linguist Wilhelm von Humboldt, a close friend of German writer Johann Wolfgang Goethe and German poet, philosopher, and dramatist Friedrich Schiller.

1871 The Industrial Revolution powers Berlin to global pre-eminence; its economy and population swell. In 1871, Berlin becomes capital of the Deutsches Reich (German Empire).

1884 The construction of the Reichstag (German Parliament) begins.

1900 Berlin's population soars to almost two million.

1914–18 World War I. Positive reactions to the war in Berlin are short lived. By the winter of 1916–17, thousands of Berliners are dependent on food aid.

1918 Military defeat in World War I and social revolution prepare the ground for the Weimar Republic, proclaimed on November 9 in Berlin. A period of political instability and inflation ensues.

1920–29 Despite economic depression, Berlin crackles with creativity during the Roaring Twenties. Cabaret, jazz, theater, and nightlife bloom.

1933 On February 27, the Reichstag is set on fire. The following day, Hitler asks for the Reichstag Fire Decree to be signed into law, which leads to the suspension of civil liberties and enables the suppression of thousands of communists and other opponents of the Nazis. As a result, the Nazis are able to increase their share of the vote (52%) in the elections on March 5. In December, Dutchman and communist Marinus van der Lubbe is convicted of arson and treason, and is beheaded the following month in Leipzig.

1936 Berlin hosts the Summer Olympic Games. The Nazi regime promotes the Aryan master race ideology. African-American track-and-field athlete Jesse Owens wins gold medals in the 100 meters, 200 meters, long jump, and 4x100-meter relay.

1938 On November 9, Jewish property and synagogues are burnt or destroyed during *Kristallnacht* (Night of the Broken Glass). Thousands of Jews from Berlin and the rest of Germany are incarcerated in concentration camps such as Sachsenhausen.

1939 Britain and France declare war on Germany.

1942 Nazi leaders convene to draft the "Final Solution" at Wannsee. This horrific plan to exterminate the Jewish people leads to the torture and murder of millions.

1945 On April 30, a defeated Hitler commits suicide together with his wife Eva Braun in his bunker underneath the Reich Chancellery on Wilhelmstrasse.

1945 On May 8, World War II officially ends. Berlin is divided into four occupation zones by Britain, France, the U.S., and the U.S.S.R.

1948 Berlin is divided into the FGR (U.S., French, and British zones) in the West and the GDR (Soviet zone) in the communist East.

1949 The U.S.S.R. sees the introduction of the Deutschmark as a breach of the Potsdam Agreement. They retaliate with the Berlin Blockade, the first major crisis of the Cold War. The allies respond with the Berlin Airlift, which delivers supplies to West Berlin.

1949 The capital of West Germany is moved from Berlin to Bonn.

1950 Stasi, Ministry for State Security and infamous spying agency, is created in the GDR. Its headquarters are located in East Berlin between Frankfurter Allee, Ruschestrasse, Normannenstrasse, and Magdalenenstrasse in Berlin-Lichtenberg.

1961 The emigration of young, skilled East Germans to the West strains the GDR economy. The Berlin Wall is built, with Soviet consent.

1963 On June 26, United States President John F. Kennedy visits West Berlin and gives a speech (p 52) on Rudolph Wilde Platz in which he famously claims, "Ich bin ein Berliner" ("I am a citizen of Berlin"). Shortly after his death in November 1963, the square is renamed John-F.-Kennedy-Platz.

1967 Berlin is twinned with Los Angeles, California.

1987 On June 12, President Ronald Reagan speaks in front of the Brandenburg Gate and challenges Soviet leader Mikhail Gorbachev to "tear down" the Berlin Wall.

1989 On November 9, Berliners celebrate the fall of the Wall.

1990 On October 3, East and West Germany are reunited, ending 45 years of Cold War division. German reunification is often referred to as *Die Wende* (the change).

1991 Berlin is again the capital of a reunified Germany.

2005 A grand coalition of the CDU–CSU (center-right Christian Democrats) and SPD (center-left Social Democrats) is elected. Angela Merkel becomes Germany's first woman chancellor.

2006 Berlin opens its new Hauptbahnhof (Central Station) and hosts the final of the FIFA Football World Cup at its Olympic Stadium.

2009 Berlin celebrates the 20th anniversary of the fall of the Wall.

Useful Phrases & Menu Terms

Useful Phrases

ENGLISH	GERMAN	PRONUNCIATION
Good day	Guten Tag	*goo*-ten taag
How are you?	Wie geht es Ihnen?	vee gait es *ee*-nen
Very well	Sehr gut	zair goot
Thank you	Danke	*dan*-ke
You're welcome	Bitte sehr	*bi*-te zair
Goodbye	Auf Wiedersehen	owf *vee*-der-zain
Please	Bitte	bi-te
Yes	Ja	yah
No	Nein	nain
Excuse me/sorry	Entschuldigung	ent-*shool*-di-gung

ENGLISH	GERMAN	PRONUNCIATION
Where is/are. . .?	Wo ist/sind. . .?	voh ist/zint
Left	Links	links
Right	Rechts	rekhts
Straight on	Geradeaus	ge-*raa*-de-ows
I would like. . .	Ich hätte gerne	ish *he*-te *ger*-ne
I want. . .	Ich möchte	ish *mer*-shte
Do you have a. . .?	Haben Sie ein. . .?	*hah*-ben zee ain
How much is it?	Wie viel kostet es?	vee feel *kos*-tet es
When?	Wann?	van
What?	Was?	vas
There is (Is there. . .?)	Es gibt (. . .gibt es?)	es gibt (. . .gibt es)
What is there?	Was gibt es?	vas gibt es
Yesterday	Gestern	*ges*-tern
Today	Heute	*hoi*-te
Tomorrow	Morgen	*mor*-gen
Good	Gut	goot
Bad	Schlecht	shlesht
Better	Besser	*be*-ser
More	Mehr	mair
Less	Weniger	*vay*-niger
Do you speak English?	Sprechen Sie Englisch?	*shpre*-khen zee *eng*-lish
I speak German	Ich spreche Deutsch	ish *shpre*-khe doitch
I don't understand	Ich verstehe nicht	ish fer-*shtaia* nisht
What is the time?	Wie viel Uhr ist es?	vee feel oor ist es
The bill, please	die Rechnung, bitte	die *resh*-nung *bi*-te
The station	der Bahnhof	dair *baan*-hof
A hotel	ein Hotel	ain ho-*tel*
The market	der Markt	dair mahrkt
A restaurant	ein Restaurant	ain res-tow-*ron*
A toilet	eine Toilette	*ai*-ne twa-*le*-te
A bank	eine Bank	*ai*-ne bank
A pharmacy	eine Apotheke	*ai*-ne a-po-tay-ke
Doctor	ein Arzt	ain artst
I'm looking for. . .	Ich suche	ish *zoo*-khe

Numbers

NUMBER	GERMAN	PRONUNCIATION
1	eins	aints
2	zwei	tsvai
3	drei	drai
4	vier	feer
5	fünf	foonf
6	sechs	zeks
7	sieben	*zee*-ben
8	acht	akht
9	neun	noin
10	zehn	tsen
11	elf	elf
12	zwölf	tsverlf

NUMBER	GERMAN	PRONUNCIATION
13	dreizehn	*drai*-tsen
14	vierzehn	*feer*-tsen
15	fünfzehn	*foonf*-tsen
16	sechzehn	*zek*-tsen
17	siebzehn	*zeeb*-tsen
18	achtzehn	*akh*-tsen
19	neunzehn	*noin*-tsen
20	zwanzig	*tsvan*-tsig
30	dreissig	*drai*-tsig
40	vierzig	*feer*-tsig
50	fünfzig	*foonf*-tsig
60	sechzig	*zek*-tsig
70	siebzig	*zeeb*-tsig
80	achtzig	*akh*-tsig
90	neunzig	*noin*-tsig
100	hundert	*hun*-dert

Days of the Week

ENGLISH	GERMAN	PRONUNCIATION
Monday	Montag	*mawn*-taak
Tuesday	Dienstag	*deens*-taak
Wednesday	Mittwoch	*mit*-vokh
Thursday	Donnerstag	*do*-ners-taak
Friday	Freitag	*frai*-taak
Saturday	Samstag	*zams*-taak
Sunday	Sonntag	*zon*-taag

Menu Savvy

ENGLISH	GERMAN	PRONUNCIATION
I would like to book a table for 8pm	Ich möchte für zwanzig Uhr einen Tisch reservieren	ish *mer*-shte foor *tsvan*-tsig oor ai-nen teesh re-zer-*vee*-ren
For two/four people	für zwei/vier Personen	foor tsvai/ feer per-*zoh*-nen
Breakfast	Frühstück	*froo*-shtook
Lunch	Mittagessen	*mi*-taak-essen
Dinner	Abendessen	*ab*-end-essen
Coffee and cake	Kaffee und Kuchen	ka-*fe* unt *koo*-khen
The menu, please	die Karte, bitte	dee *kaar*-te *bi*-te
Waiter/waitress	Herr Ober/Fräulein	hair *oh*-ber/*froy*-lein
A knife	ein Messer	ain *me*-sser
A fork	eine Gabel	*ai*-ne *gah*-bel
A spoon	ein Löffel	ain *loo*-fel
A cup	eine Tasse	*ai*-ne *ta*-sse
A glass	ein Glas	ain glahs
A plate	ein Teller	ain *te*-lair
A bowl	eine Schüssel	*ai*-ne *shoo*-sel

Index

See also Accommodations and Restaurant indexes, below.

Photo **Credits**